MARRIA___
INDEXES
for Family Historians

NINTH (2008) EDITION

Jeremy Gibson,
Elizabeth Hampson and Stuart Raymond

The Family History Partnership

Ninth edition published by
The Family History Partnership,
PO Box 502,
Bury, Lancashire BL8 9EP.

Email: sales@thefamilyhistorypartnership.com
Webpage: www.thefamilyhistorypartnership.com

Earlier editions published under varying titles by the
Federation of Family History Societies.

Eighth edition, as *Marriage and Census Indexes for Family Historians*, 2000.

Ninth edition, as *Marriage Indexes for Family Historians*,
Copyright © Jeremy Gibson, 2007.

ISBN 978 1 906280 03 1

Typeset from computer disks prepared by Jeremy Gibson and Elizabeth Hampson.
Printed by the Alden Press, Witney, Oxfordshire.

Acknowledgments

This Guide was originally an amalgamation of *Marriage Indexes: How To Find Them; How to Use Them; How to Compile Them,* and of *Census Indexes and Indexing.* The former was the idea of the late Michael Walcot, whilst Colin Chapman was a pioneer of census indexing. The proliferation of indexes of both sorts is a tribute to my co-editors in these guides.

For six editions the Guide included 'Specialist Indexes', but their ever increasing number has meant that these have now been split off and appear in a separate Guide, of which a third edition should appear shortly. John Perkins developed *Current Publications by Member Societies* and its companion *Current Publications on Microfiche by Member Societies* (see page 5). The latest edition was produced by my co-compiler Elizabeth Hampson, which has made her collaboration in this Guide even more knowledgeable and valuable. Information from these has been cross-checked, but inevitably it may be out-of-date by the time this new edition appears. The same goes for internet websites and addresses. Users are therefore recommended to cross-refer where possible. We are always glad to hear of new indexes.

Such have been developments in the seven years since the last edition that it has been necessary to separate Marriages Indexes from those to Censuses once again. Though for both types of index the internet is now the first port of call, nationwide Census Indexes are well-known. Marriage Indexes remain in general the initiative of family history societies and individuals, though most have internet websites and email addresses

Marriage indexers have mostly been prompt to reply to enquiries. We are most grateful to them for their help, and hope this Guide will continue to make their indexes known in the way they wish. It is only fair to them to mention that the conditions of use printed in this Guide may be changed by them at any time with no obligation to inform anyone beforehand.

The information provided here has been gathered over several years, delayed by personal problems now overcome. As with the previous edition, the bulk of the work of gathering, sorting and typing has been undertaken by Elizabeth Hampson, whilst Stuart Raymond's familiarity with the intrnet has been invaluable. My own contribution has mainly been restircted to the final arrangement of the text.

J.S.W.G.

CONTENTS

3

PREFACE

This Guide is arranged in the order of the historic (pre-1974) counties of England and Wales, followed by Scotland and Ireland, and off-shore islands..

Under most counties there are references to Boyd's and Pallot's Marriage Indexes. Details of these are given on page 6.

The nature of the indexes has changed since the Guide first appeared, and now many are published. Most published marriage indexes are included. For a fuller range consult *Current Publications...* (page 5). Marriage indexes to individual places are generally omitted.

Internet websites and email addresses are by their nature constantly changing and easy to mistype. Corrections, alterations and additions will be welcomed by Jeremy Gibson at Harts Cottage, Church Hanborough, Witney, Oxon. OX29 8AB.

How to Use these Indexes

When requesting a search in any of the following indexes it is essential to:

1. Apply by *E-mail*, or *letter* if that is not available, not in person or by telephone.

2. If applying by letter, enclose a self-addressed envelope, stamped in the UK (SAE) and the minimum fee requested in the form of a postal order or postage stamps (for convenience at current 1st or 2nd class rate). UK users should make out cheques to the society or individual specified. If this is unclear it is best to leave the payee unentered (now that most cheques specify 'Account Payee' and endorsement is impossible). Overseas users should send at least two International Reply Coupons (Australian and New Zealand users should send three coupons) and Sterling banknotes or postal orders (*e.g.* in New Zealand); if no Sterling banknotes are available, then banknotes of the country concerned large enough to cover postage, search cost and at least ten per cent extra for conversion charge. Do *not* send coins. If a personal cheque or money order is sent this should be in Sterling on a corresponding bank in London or in local currency with at least the equivalent of £15 extra to cover the conversion charges. Sterling is always preferable.

3. Offer to send a donation, if no fee is stipulated, and particularly if a list is expected. Professional users should invariably send a donation or increased fee.

4. If by letter, leave space for the reply to be written. This can then be returned to you, saving stationery, explanation and time.

5. If an index is run in association with a family history society, consider joining that society (if not already a member).

Abbreviations

Most abbreviations used are common and well known.

BT	= Bishop's Transcript(s)	o.p.	= out of print
FHS	= Family History Society	p&p	= postage and packing
IRC	= International Reply Coupon	PR	= Parish Register(s)
m'fche	= microfiche	SAE	= stamped addressed envelope

GENERAL MARRIAGE INDEXES

General Register Office Indexes. This immensely important set of indexes, from July 1837 for England and Wales, is described in all genealogical textbooks. See *The National Achives: a practical guide for family historians*, by Stella Colwell, The National Archives, 2006. Microfilm sets of the indexes are held in a number of libraries outside London. For Scottish and Irish civil registers, see under the entries for those countries.

A free search facility to the old index is provided by FreeBMD at **<freebmd.rootsweb.com>**. This is not complete as yet. Coverage is given on the site. The full index is available on a number of commercial sites; these include:
<www.192.com/Genealogy>
<www.ancestry.co.uk>
<www.bmdindex.co.uk>
<www.familyrelatives.com>
<www.findmypast.com>
<www.thegenealogist.co.uk>

The GRO is currently re-indexing its civil registers. The new database will be available on-line in a year or two. Meanwhile it seems that access to these will be difficult.

Details are available at **<www.gro.gov.uk>**

Many Family History Societies are creating indexes from the registers held by district registrars, in an attempt to avoid many of the mistakes that were made in the G.R.O. indexes. These are slowly becoming available online, and are listed under counties below. A full listing is online at:
<www.ukbmd.org.uk/index.php>

Original Parish Registers, copies, indexes, etc. These are listed in detail in the county volumes of the *National Index of Parish Registers*, published by the Society of Genealogists. Volumes currently available, visit:
<www.sog.org.uk/acatalog/National_Index_of_ Parish_Registers.html>

The Phillimore Atlas and Index of parish registers, ed. Cecil R. Humphery-Smith (3rd ed. Phillimore, 2003), provides a summary listing of original parish registers, togther with maps of parish boundaries juxtaposed with 19th century county maps.

Published Transcripts and Indexes of Parish Registers. Regular reference is made throughout this Guide to transcripts and indexes published by FHSs. These are listed in much greater detail in *Current Publications on Microfiche by Member Societies*, 5th ed. FFHS, 2002 by John P. Perkins; and *Current Publications by Member Societies*, 10th ed. FFHS, 1999 by Elizabeth Hampson. FHS websites usually list their own publications; many can also be identified at **<www.genfair.com>**, and at **<www.parishchest.com>**.

A number of other organizatons have also published, and sometimes indexed, many parish registers. *Phillimore's parish register series* includes registers (mainly marriage) from *c*.1,400 parishes, which are listed in M. Bryant-Rosier, *Index to parishes in Phillimore's marriages* (Family Tree Magazine, 1988). The Parish Register Society printed over 100 registers, as did the Harleian Society (webpage:
<fmg.ac/Harleian/Volumes.htm>)
- the latter mainly (but not solely) for London. A variety of local parish register publishers are listed under appropriate counties below.

These published transcripts and indexes are listed in the county volumes of Stuart Raymond's series of genealogical bibliographies. These are mentioned under the appropriate counties below. Many published registers have been re-issued on CD. These are listed in Raymond's *British family history on CD*, 2001. For other useful publications, consult his *English genealogy: a bibliography*, 3rd ed., 1996.

Thousands of parish registers have been transcribed and indexed on the internet. In general, individual registers on the internet are not listed here. A full listing is provided by S.A. Raymond, *Births marriages and deaths on the web: a directory*. 2 vols. 2nd ed. FFHS, 2005.

The works by Perkins, Hanson and Raymond noted above should be available at your local FHS bookstall. Although originally published by the Federation of Family History Societies, information is not currently available (late 2007) on sales outlets to replace the former depot. The publishers of this edition, The Family History Partnership, stock all Raymond and Gibson publications, on:
<www.familyhistorypartnership.co.uk>
or try Webpage: **<www.genfair.com>**

Society of Genealogists. See its leaflet, *Using the Library of the Society of Genealogists* (also available on the website). This describes many of the indexes in the Society's possession. These include: IGI for christenings and marriages worldwide with most events 1538-*c*.1875. Indexes to B.C.M. in the Scottish OPRs 1553-1855. Vital Records Index (VRI) for christenings and marriages in the British Isles 1538-1888.

Civil registration of births, marriages and deaths: GRO indexes to births, marriages and deaths in England and Wales 1837-1925 (including overseas, military, naval and air returns up to *c*.1965).

Scottish GRO indexes to births, marriages and deaths 1855-1920.

Many published indexes to parish registers, marriage licences, etc., covering the whole country.

Society of Genealogists, 14 Charterhouse Buildings, Goswell Road, London EC1M 7BA
Website: **<www.sog.org.uk>**

Family History Online. Numerous marriage indexes compiled by FHS's are hosted on this site. Most are listed under the appropriate county below - but it may pay to check recent updates on the site. <www.familyhistoryonline.org.uk>

International Genealogical Index. This microfiche index, prepared by the Genealogical Society of the Church of Jesus Christ of LatterDay Saints, is now widely available in libraries, record offices and family history centres. It is also available on their own web site, and also on CD (as the *British Isles vital records index*).
Webpage: <**www.familysearch.org/**>

Bernau's Marriage Index. An index to all marriages printed in the 200 volumes of marriage register transcripts published by Phillimore & Co. Ltd. for which there are no index volumes, compiled by Charles Bernau. Enquiries SAE/2 IRCs
Pinhorns, 85 Etnam Street, Leominster HR6 8AE.

Boyd's Marriage Index. This is available in its entirety at the *Society of Genealogists.* Seven million English marriages 1538-1837; in typescript volumes on open shelves. Fees payable for use by non-members (£3.50 an hour; £9.20, for any four hours; or £14.50 for the day (the daily fee includes the evening on Thursday). Open 10am to 6pm Tues. to Sat. and until 8pm on Thurs.). A microfiche copy is at the *Institute of Heraldic and Genealogical Studies (Northgate, Canterbury, Kent CT1 1BA),* where it can be examined at the library rate. Its coverage is given in *A List of Parishes in Boyd's Marriage Index,* published by the Society, and in *The Phillimore Atlas and Index of Parish Registers.* Coverage is noted below under each county. The index is also available online, pay per view.
Website: <**www.britishorigins.com/help/popup-aboutbo-bmi2.htm**>

Freereg aims to provide free internet searches of parish registers for the British Isles. It is far from complete, and needs volunteers.
Webpage: <**www.freereg.org.uk**>

The Joiner Marriage Index: a Marriage Index for the North of England covers many parishes in Cumberland, Derbyshire, Co.Durham, Hertfordshire, Leicestershire, Lincolnshire, Northumberland, Nottinghamshire, Westmorland and Yorkshire. Leaflet giving details with up to date parish dates available for a SAE or by email request. Complete date, parish of origin and widows shown for about 75% of the entries. Searches undertaken for £5.00 per enquiry. One surname requests answered providing the name is not too numerous. The database is also available online at:
<**www.joinermarriageindex.co.uk**>
Paul R. Joiner, Greystones, The Spital, Yarm-on-Tees, Yorkshire TS15 9EX.

Birth, Marriage and Death Certificates *(BMSGH).* Index of names on unwanted certificates. Online pay--per-view index, see under Warws., page 28.

Pallot's Marriage Index. One of the most important and useful indexes of marriages. For those whose ancestry is lost in London before General Registration this is an essential source. It covers all but two of the 103 ancient parishes of the old City of London for the period 1780-1837, with entries taken from original sources, many now lost. The index has been augmented by entries from other counties, usually transcribed from printed sources. There was an equivalent baptismal section but this was severely damaged during the Second World War; however, some 100,000 entries survive. A CD of the Index is available through the IHGS online shop. Non-members may visit the library at a daily rate of £18.00 (including VAT). Space in the library is limited. All members and visitors must make an appointment with the librarian so that it can be ensured that there is enough room for all who so wish to work without interruption or discomfort. Library hours are Sunday and Monday closed all day. Tues, Wed, Fri and Sat 10am-6pm and Thursday 10am-8pm. For more information, please contact the Librarian on (01227 768664).
Institute of Heraldic and Genealogical Studies, Northgate, Canterbury, Kent. CT1 1BA
Webpage: <**www.ihgs.ac.uk**>

The Catholic Central Library has deposited copies of register transcripts, which, combined with registers published by the Catholic Record Society, make a very full collection of London Catholic Registers up to 1850. Also deposited with the library are:
• registers from parts of Carmarthen Wales, and Berks, Bucks, Cornwall, Devon, Dorset, Durham, Essex, Lancs, Northumb, Notts, Somerset, Staffs, Warwicks, Wilts, Worc.
• 'The Midlands District Confirmation Register', 1768-1815, covering 15 counties
Catholic National Library, St Michael's Abbey, Farnborough Road, Farnborough, Hants GU14 7NQ.
Webpage: <**www.catholic-library.org.uk/**>
email: librarian@catholic-library.org.uk

JewishGen UK Database. Its marriage index includes 3,500 records covering 1838 to 1972, from all areas of the U.K., including West London Synagogue, 1842-1952 (2,608 records). Webpage:
<**www.jewishgen.org/databases/UK/**>

Marriage Licence Allegations Index 1694-1850: Vicar-General and Faculty Office. Online database available (pay per view) on British Origins webpage:
<**www.britishorigins.com/help/popup-aboutbo-mla.htm**>

Emigration.
Published indexes to births, marriages, and deaths in Australia and New Zealand up to about 1900.
Society of Genealogists, 14 Charterhouse Buildings, Goswell Road, London EC1M 7BA.
Webpage: <**www.sog.org.uk**>

BEDFORDSHIRE

Published Registers *(Beds FHS)* Bedfordshire is unique in having had all its parish registers to 1812 published. They were originally published as books, and can be found in many libraries. They are now available on m'fiche from Beds FHS.

Bedfordshire Parish Registers Index (Master Edition*) (Beds FHS)* This database is a single consolidated surname index of all entries in the 128 Bedfordshire Parish Registers up to 1812. It can be searched to lead you to the pages in the register transcripts, which you will then need to consult in printed form or on microfiche to see detailed entries. **Indexes of Marriages Licences**. *(Beds FHS)*. Marriage Licences 1747-1790; Marriage Licences 1578-1618 and 1791-1812; Marriage Licences 1813-1848; Marriage Licences 1848-1885. 4 vols in total. *Bedfordshire FHS, PO Box 214, Bedford, MK42 9RX*
email: *searches@bfhs.org.uk*
Website: **<www.bfhs.org.uk/>**
(click on 'publications list')
Beds FHS publications are also available from **<www.genfair.com>** and **<www.parishchest.co.uk>**

Bedfordshire and Luton Archives. IGI covers all but 12 parishes to 1812, and some to 1837 or 1875. The remaining parishes (and others omitted from IGI) on card index to 1812. Thus the whole county is covered to 1812 except for Quakers and Jews. **Marriage Licences** *only*. Covers **1578-1618, 1747-1885.** [Some early gaps]. Index to 1812 pub. in Beds. Parish Registers Series Vols 14 and 15. Index 1813-1885, typescript in Bedfordshire and Luton Archives and Records Service.
County Archivist, Bedfordshire and Luton Archives and Record Service, County Hall, Cauldwell Street, Bedford MK42 9AP.
Webpage: **<www.Bedfordshire.gov.uk/archive>**

Boyd. In Miscellaneous Series, 8 parishes only.

Pallot. 43 parishes.

BERKSHIRE
(Vale of the White Horse now in Oxfordshire)

Berkshire Marriage Index (BMI); Berkshire Burial Index (BBI); Berks FHS Strays Index; Berkshire Miscellaneous Berkshire Census (1851, 1861, 1871).
The Berkshire Name Search allows information from various Society records to be searched and accessed. A search of the master index, the Berkshire Miscellaneous Index, will show the number of entries of that name in the individual datasets (indexes). You can then request the full details available: these are full transcriptions of the census entries and lesser transcriptions for burial and marriage indexes. The reliability of the records is indicated and ranges from records from third parties to those checked against original records.

Postal search charges are (a) £2 per surname to search the master Berkshire Name Index and be advised on the number of entries in each data set. This search will not provide information from the records. and/or (b) £2 per surname per database or £5 for all the databases currently available. Both will give full details for up to a maximum of 25 entries. We will advise the extra cost if more entries. The £5 charge for multiple datasets may be increased when more datasets are available. Please enclose an A4 sized SAE (or IRC) or give us your e-mail address for the results to be sent to you by email. Please note the date of your search so that future searches need only cover and charge for additions to the Berkshire Name Search since your previous search.
Berkshire Name Search, Berkshire FHS Research Centre, Yeomanry House, 131 Castle Hill, Reading RG1 7TJ, United Kingdom.
email: *BerksNameSearch@BerksFHS.org.uk*

The Berkshire FHS's **Berkshire Marriage index** is also available on-line at two pay-per-view sites, both of which include full details of the parishes covered:
<www.berksfhs.org.uk/berkshire/ BerkshireMarriageIndex.htm>
<www.familyhistoryonline.net/database/ BRKMarriageIndex.shtml>

Berkshire Marriage Index. *(compiled by the late J.W. Brooks)*. Complete coverage of the ancient county, with some adjacent parishes in other counties, males only to 1837. 95% original registers, 3% BTs. 2% checked transcripts. All register details, excluding witnesses. Widows shown, alphabetical order. Fee £3.50 per specific marriage enquiry, extended enquiries or limited lists by arrangement. SAE or 4 IRC's please. Stray marriage contributions are much appreciated. Also available: some marriage Licences for Berkshire and Oxford archdeaconry. Salisbury licences, peculiars. Also approx 5,000 stray Berks marriages. Cheques to:
Mrs P. Knight, Old Oak Cottage, The Pound, Cookham, Maidenhead, Berks. SL6 9QE.

Berkshire Record Office.
General Register Office indexes up to 2000.
A microfilm copy of **John Brooks' marriage index** (see page 7) is held. It is suspected to be based on inaccurate transcription and may be incomplete.
Berkshire R.O. 9 Coley Avenue, Reading RG1 6AF.
email: *ARCH@reading.gov.uk*
Web site: <**www.berkshirerecordoffice.org.uk**>

North Berkshire 1538-1851 *(Oxfordshire FHS).* Covers most of that part of North Berkshire in present day Oxfordshire. Computer searches as under Oxfordshire, page ?.
Dr. Alan Simpson, Forest Farmhouse, Old Road, Shotover Hill, Headington, Oxford OX3 8TA
Webpage:
<**searches.oxfordshirefhs.org.uk/#marrs**>

Berkshire Marriages 1538-1837 *(Oxfordshire Record Office),* on 16mm m'film, index by groom only.
Oxfordshire Record Office, St Luke's Church, Temple Road, Cowley, Oxford OX4 2HT.
email: *Archives @Oxfordshire.gov.uk*

Marriage Licence Bonds for Sarum Diocese 1609-1837 (incl. Wiltshire, Berkshire and Dorset). Publication on CD from Wiltshire FHS. see page 20

Boyd. In Miscellaneous Series. 13 parishes.

Pallot. 13 parishes.

BUCKINGHAMSHIRE

Published Registers. Many published registers are listed in S.A. Raymond, *Buckinghamshire: a genealogical bibliography.* FFHS, 1993.

Buckinghamshire Marriage Database (Bucks FHS). The Society's Marriages Database contains all available register entries for marriages which took place in Buckinghamshire between 1538 and 1837 (over 170,000 marriages). Full county search for a specific marriage: £1 plus self-addressed A5 envelope and UK 1st class stamp. Search for every reference to a surname for any 100 year period: £2 plus self addressed A4 envelope and 3 loose UK 1st class stamps. Searches of the database can be made by contacting:
Bucks FHS Marriage Searches, P.O. Box 403, Aylesbury, Bucks HP21 7GU.
email: *marriages@bucksfhs.org.uk•*
webpage: <**www.bucksfhs.org.uk**>
(click 'database searches' and 'marriage searches'

Buckinghamshire Marriages *(Bucks FHS).* 32,319 entries from 36 parish registers (with some BTs) mainly covering the period from the start of the registers to 1901. Online, pay per view. The data is taken from registers published by Bucks FHS (see below)
Webpage:
<**www.familyhistoryonline.net/database** BucksFHSmar.shtml>

CD Publications.*(Bucks FHS):*
Aylesbury, St Mary. CMB 1565-1901;
Penn, Holy Trinity CMB 1559-1901
Beaconsfield, St Mary CM 1575-1901 Burials 1540-1901.
Parishes on disk and in printed form.
Gawcott Bap 1806-1901, Burials 1807-1867; Dunton CMB 1577-1901; Halton C1663-1901, MB 1604-1900; The Lee CB 1671-1901, M 1700-1901.
Hoggeston CMB 1548-1901;Taplow CMB 1605-1901; Taplow CMB 1605-1901; Granborough CMB 1538-1901; Addington CMB 1559-1901; Ashendon CMB 1590-1901; Thornborough CMB 1601-1901; Westcott CMB 1867-1901; Hedsor CMB 1678-1901; Chearsley CMB 1571-1901; Hedgerley CMB 1539-1901; Grove C 1596-1899, M 1606-1899, B 1839-1901.
Bucks. FHS Sales, Joyce Kendell, PO Box 403, Aylesbury HP21 7GU.
Webpage: <**www.bucksfhs.org.uk**>
(click 'online shop' and 'parish registers').

McLaughlin Index *(Buckinghamshire Genealogical Society).* Now complete. **Marriages basically 1538-1837,** many strays identified outside their county. For more contact:
Antony McLaughlin, Varneys, Rudds Lane, Haddenham, Bucks. HP17 8JP.
email: *kevin.quick@bucksgs.org.uk*
Webpage: <**www.bucksgs.org.uk**>

Buckinghamshire Banns of Marriage. This index consists of 2,898 entries from 35 parishes mainly covering the period from the start of the registers to 1901. The entries are from the Church of England parish registers.
Website:
<**www.familyhistoryonline.net/database/** BucksFHSbann.shtml>

Boyd. In Miscellaneous Series, 64 parishes, approx. 30% of county.

Pallot. 68 parishes.

CAMBRIDGESHIRE

CAMDEX Online Records. Online index to civil registers held by District registrars. In progress. **<www.cambridgeshire.gov.uk/community/bmd/Camdex/>**

Cambridgeshire. Covers those parishes and periods not in Boyd.
1801-1837 (by the late T.P.R. Layng). Complete except Thorney. Arrangement as Boyd but not fully phonetic. Copies also at *Huntingdon R.O.* and at *Society of Genealogists.*
1754-1800. Card Index. Complete except Thorney. Arranged under males. Complete date and parish of domicile. Widows shown. Not fully phonetic.
1626-1675 *(Cambs. FHS).* Complete arrangement etc. as Boyd to cover the period which, for Cambs., is in Boyd's general series.
1538-1754. Card index covering omissions in Boyd, other details as above.
For Thorney see Huntingdonshire.
Cambridgeshire Archives and Local Studies, Box RES 1009, Shire Hall, Castle Hill, Cambridge CB3 0AP.

Cambridge College Marriage Registers 1695-1837, indexed transcript (published: Cambridge Univ. Heraldic and Genealogical Society). Copies available from:
D.A. Palgrave, Crossfield House, Dale Road, Stanton, Bury St. Edmunds, Suffolk IP31 2DY.

A Marriage Index for the County *(Cambridgeshire FHS)* is an on-going project - as parishes are computerised, they are added to the index and updates are produced regularly. These indexes are all available as searchable CDs, and also online (pay-view) at
<www.familyhistoryonline.net/database/CambsFHSmar.shtml>
Individual parishes can be purchased on m'fiche. Visit **<www.cfhs.org.uk/bookstall.html>** or **<www.genfair.com>** for details of CDs and fiche available. All transcripts available from:
C and P Noble, 22 St. Margaret's Road, Girton, Cambridge CB3 0LY.

Boyd. In Main Series and some in Miscellaneous. 170 parishes and one Meeting for the Society of Friends. Approx. 99% of county. Nearly all parishes, except those in the Deanery of Fordham, have BT entries as well as those from original registers. The whole of 1626-1675 is in the Miscellaneous Series. Copy of Cambs. Boyd (excl. 1626-1675) at *County Record Offices, Cambridge* and *Huntingdon.*

Pallot. 44 parishes.

Cambridgeshire Banns of Marriage. Indexes 53,857 banns of marriage from 74 parishes and other places in the county of Cambridgeshire.
Webpage: **<www.familyhistoryonline.net/database/CambsFHSbanns.shtml>**

CHESHIRE

Published Registers. Many published registers are listed in S.A. Raymond, *Cheshire: a genealogical bibliography. Vol.1. Cheshire genealogical sources.* FFHS., 1995.

Cheshire BMD: Births, Marriages and Deaths on the Internet. Online index to District Registrar's registers, 1837-1950, in progress.
Webpage: **<cheshirebmd.org.uk>**

Cheshire Marriage Index, 1650-1837. Males only. In four period divisions **(1650-1700; 1701-1755; 1756-1800; 1801-1837)**. Over 90,000 entries, still in progress. 5% from printed sources. Mainly from BT's inc. some Welsh border BTs held at Chester. Complete date. Widows shown. Alphabetical. Available on m'fche **1701-1837**.
Bertram Merrell, 3912 South 2520 West, West Valley City, Utah 84119, U.S.A.

Bertram Merrell's Index of **Marriage Licenses, Allegations and Bonds**, in the **Chester Diocese 1750-1837** covering south Lancashire, Cheshire and parts of Flintshire, Denbighshire and Yorkshire. About 50,000 entries of intentions to marry and many recording ages, whether widow or widower, parentage and intended church or chapelry. Looking for the whereabouts of a name, or if a marriage was by license then a search can be made in the Index by writing to Bertram Merrell as above. This index is also available on CD, from
<www.fhsc.org.uk/fhsc/cdrom.htm>

Cheshire Marriage Index *(FHS of Cheshire).* Available on CD (only Windows 95/98), this covers 150,000 marriages in almost all of Cheshire parishes, from 1700 onwards. Both bride and groom's surnames can be searched.
CD Sales: Mr Colin Dutton, 5 Haydock Close, Tytherington, Macclesfield SK10 2WG.
<www.fhsc.org.uk/fhsc/cdrom.htm>
email: *cd.sales@fhsc.org.uk*

North and East Cheshire. Complete 1754-1837 for eastern half of county 40% pre-1754 for same area. Both parties to 1837 from PRs, BTs and printed sources. Over 250,000 marriages. Alphabetical, some phonetic insertions. Widows shown. Specific enquiry, SAE + £1 donation.
Mrs P.M. Litton, 2 Florence Road, Harrogate, North Yorks. HG2 0LD.
CD available from *FHS of Cheshire* as above.

The North Wales Marriage Index Part 5: The Marches. 21 ancient and three modern parishes bordering on and around the Welsh border. As Flintshire. *Dafydd Hayes,* page 32.

Boyd. 18 parishes in Miscellaneous Series.

Pallot. 9 parishes.

Cheshire continued

Marriage Indexes at C.R.O. Barrow 1590-1880 (G. Lea); Bidston 1581-1700 (C. Bratt); Davenham 1700-1900 (Cheshire FHS, Northwich Group); Harthill 1599-1837 (P.M. Litton); Siddington 1722-1783; Stockport 1799-1837; West Kirby 1692-1729 (C. Bratt). Hard copy index for the Chester R.D. 1837-1856 (will be supplemented in future years).

Bertram Merrell's Marriage Index 1750-1837 (period covered varies with individual parishes).

Hartley Jones Marriage Index to the Wirral, 1580-1850.

North and East Cheshire Marriage Index 1754-1837.

Cheshire Record Office, Duke St, Chester CH1 1RL.
Webpage:
<www.cheshire.gov.uk/recoff/home.htm>

North Cheshire FHS Publications.
Macclesfield St Michael Marriages 1699-1754.

Great Budworth, Allostock Unitarian Marriages [includes Christenings and Burials] 1690-1823.

Stockport St Mary Marriages, 1584-1629, 1629-1754.

Cherford St John's Marriages 1674-1752 [includes Baptisms 1673-1849]. Available from:
Mrs Rhoda Clarke, 2 Denham Drive, Bramhall, Stockport Cheshire SK7 2 AT.
Webpage: **<www.ncfhs.org.uk/>**

Marriage (Licences and Bonds) 1639-1765.
Webpage: **<www.geocities.com/fountalnpen/marriages2.html>**

Chester Marriage Licence Bonds February-[April] 1825
Webpage: **<homepages.rootsweb.com/~mwi/che1825f.txt>**
Continued as follows:
1825 May-August **</che1825m.txt>**
1825 December **</che1825d.txt>**
1826 January **</che1826j.txt>**

See also Lancashire.

CORNWALL

Published Parish Registers. Many published registers are listed in S.A. Raymond, *Cornwall: a genealogical bibliography.* 2nd ed. FFHS, 1994. Some were issued by Devon and Cornwall Record Society.

Cornwall 1538-1837 *(Cornwall FHS)* 100% coverage, indexed by male and female, members send SAE/2IRCs for surname estimate.
Cornwall FHS, 5 Victoria Square, Truro, Cornwall TR1 2RS.
Webpage (listing parishes covered):
<www.cornwallfhs.com/pdf/MarriageParishTotals>
This index is also available online, pay-per-view.
Website: **<www.familyhistoryonline.net/database/CONMarriageIndex.shtml>**

Cornwall continued

Publications from *Cornwall FHS.*
Marriages Pre-1813. An index of Marriages from Phillimore, Taylor *et al.*
Marriages 1813 - 1837. An index of Marriages from 1813 to 1837
Marriages Pre-Civil An index of Marriages pre-civil marriages, any gaps in the Parish Registers have tried to be filled in with entries in the Bishops Transcripts.
Cornwall Family History Society, 5 Victoria Square, Truro Cornwall TR1 2RS.
email: *enquiries@cornwallfhs.comemail orders@cornwallfhs.com*
Webpage: **<www.cornwallfhs.com/>**

Cornish 19th century marriages recorded in parish registers are indexed online at
<www.geocities.com/ausich2000>

Boyd. In Main Series, 206 parishes, approx. 93% of the county. All BTs from 1597-1673 are included. A copy of this Index is in the possession of the *Devon and Cornwall Record Society.* No postal enquiries, conditions as for Fursdon index (see under *Devon*).

Pallot. 148 parishes.

CUMBERLAND
(part of Cumbria)

Published Registers. Many published parish registers are listed in S.A. Raymond, *Cumberland and Westmorland: a genealogical bibliography.* FFHS, 1993.

Cumberland Pre-1813 marriages except when shown otherwise: Addingham, Aikton, Ainstable, Allhallows, Alston, Arlecdon (pre-1838), Arthuret (pre-1837), Aspatria, Bassenthwaite, Beaumont, Bewcastle (pre 1839), Bolton, Bowness-on-Solway, Brampton (pre 1839), Bridekirk, Bromfield, Burgh-by-Sands, Caldbeck, Camerton, Carlisle St. Cuthbert, Carlisle St. Mary, Castle Carrock, Castle Sowerby, Croglin (pre-1837), Crosby on Eden (pre 1839), Crosscanonby (pre 1838), Crosthwaite, Culgaith, Cumrew (pre-1838), Cumwhitton (pre-1838), Dacre, Dalston, Dearham (pre-1838), Edenhall, Egremont (pre-1838), Ennerdale, Eskdale, Farlam (pre 1839), Flimby, Garrigill, Gilcrux (pre-1838), Gosforth (also 1837-1915), Great Orton, Great Salkeld, Greystoke, Grinsdale, Hayton, Hesket in the Forest, Holme Cultram (1838-1871), Holme St Cuthbert's 1850-1900, Home St Paul's (1850-1900) Hutton in the Forest, Ireby, Irthington, Isel, Kirkandrews on Esk (pre-1838), Kirkbampton, Kirkbride, Kirkland, Kirklinton, Kirkoswald, Lamplugh, Lanercost (1837-1952) (and 1837-1952), Langwathby, Lazonby, Maryport (pre-1838), Matterdale (pre 1837), Melmerby, Millom (pre-1839), Muncaster (pre-1838), Nether Denton (pre 1839), Newton Reigny, Nicholforest, Ousby,

Over Denton (pre 1839), Penrith (pre-1770 and 1837-1966), Plumbland, Raughton Head, Renwick (pre-1838), Rockcliffe (pre 1838), St. Bees (pre-1838), Scaleby, Sebergham, Skelton, Stanwix (pre 1838), Stapleton (pre 1838), Threlkeld, Thursby (pre-1838), Torpenhow (to 1812 only), Uldale, Waberthwaite, Walton, Warwick (pre 1839), Warwick Bridge R.C. Church 1769-1900), Wasdale (1721-1840), Watermillock, Westnewton (1862-1978)Westward (pre-1838), Wetheral, Whicham, Whitehaven Holy Trinity and St. Nicholas (both pre-1838), Wigton.
Widows not shown. Alphabetical. No fees but only limited searching.
Cumbria Record Office, The Castle, Carlisle CA3 8UR.

Ramsden Marriage Index for South Cumberland 1650-1813. Prepared in association with *Cumbria FHS.* Beckermet St. Bridget's,Beckermet St John's. Bootle, Corney, Drigg, Ennerdale, Eskdale, Gosforth, Haile, Irton, Millom, Muncaster, Netherwasdale, Ponsonby, Thwaites, Ulpha, Waberthwaite, Wasdale Head, Whicham and Whitbeck.
Cumbria R.O. and Local Studies Library, 140 Duke St., Barrow-in-Furness, LA14 1XW.
email: *barrow.record.office@cumbriacc.gov.uk*

Cumberland Marriages 1813-1839. *Brampton Deanery.* A full series of baptism, marriage and burial indexes for parishes and chapelries in Cumberland for 1813-1839 are available on CD. Write for list incl. Originally published by *Original Indexes,* but now available from *Ancestral Indexes eShop* (run by *Northumberland and Durham FHS*)
Webpage: **<www.ancestral-indexes.co.uk>**

Calendar of Diocese of Carlisle Marriage Licences/Bond 1668-1824 in 8 vols, all separately indexed. *Volumes 1-3 (1668-1762) published by Cumbria FHS and Cumbria Archive Service.*

Barrow-in-Furness, St George's, 1861-1880 (3 card index drawers in search room).

Geldart Marriage Index of South Cumberland. A-M only, males, 16th-19th centuries, approx. 22 parishes, but virtually superseded by the Ramsden index.
The above indexes are at *Cumbria R.O. and Local Studies Library, as above.*

Cumberland BMD 1775-c1855. Pacquet. 55 drawers.
Daniel Hay Library, Whitehaven.

Boyd. In Main and Miscellaneous Series, 35 parishes (mostly pre-1700). Approx 20% of county.

Joiner. 25,760 entries from 26 parishes.

Pallot. 17 parishes.

CUMBRIA
See Cumberland, Lancashire *and* Westmorland.

DERBYSHIRE

Published Registers. Some registers are available on CD, from two separate publishers. Visit the websites of Valerie Neal and Ancestral Archives:
<www.genuki.org.uk/big/eng/DBY/ValNealCDs.html>
<www.genuki.org.uk/big/eng/DBY/AncestralArchives.html>

Derbyshire Marriage Index. Males only, to 1837. 1538-1812, 90% of the county; 1813-1837, virtually complete. Original registers, BTs and printed sources used. Complete date. Phonetic. Similar names supplied. List available. Specific marriages only, no blanket searches or block extracts. No fee but SAE essential, donations welcome.
Miss Sue Brown, 25 Homecroft Drive, Packington, Ashby de la Zouch, Leics LE65 1WG.

Chesterfield Parish Church Registers 1553-1812. *(Chesterfield and Dist FHS.)* Card index to the registers 1558-1812, also a printed index of brides and grooms for **St Peter and Paul's** church at **Old Brampton 1756-1945.**
Chesterfield Local Studies Library, New Beetwell Street, Chesterfield.

Derby Marriages. A name index that includes some from Phillimores. Many parish registers now transcribed and available for research on CD. Searchable by name.
Derby Local Studies Library, 25b Iron Gate, Derby DE22 1FS.
email: *localstudies.library@derby.gov.uk*

Derbyshire Registrar's Marriage Index *(Derbyshire FHS).* Index of RD's civil registers, in progress. Available online at
<www.familyhistoryonline.net/database/DBYRegMarrIndex.shtml>
Postal inquiries should be directed to:
The DFHS, Bridge Chapel House, St.Mary's Bridge, Sowter Rd., Derby DE1 3AT.
Webpage:
<www.dfhs.org.uk/searches/dfhsschs.htm>

Phillimore Marriages. 39 printed transcripts of Derbyshire parish registers published by Phillimore have been digitised at UK-Genealogy Archives webpage:
<www.uk-genealogy.org.uk/Registers/index.html>

Boyd. In Main Series. 80 parishes, approx. 40% of the county.

Joiner. 80 parishes; 82954 entries.

Pallot. 76 parishes.

DEVON

Published Registers. Many published registers are listed in S.A. Raymond, *Devon: a genealogical bibliography. Vol.1. Devon genealogical sources.* 2nd ed. FFHS, 1994. Some were published by the Devon and Cornwall Record Society.

Marriage Index 1754-1812 Complete for Devon.
Marriage Index 1813-1837 Complete for Devon.
Plymouth Marriages post 1837, 41 Church of England parishes (Volume 1).
Plymouth Marriages post 1837, 95. Church of England, non-conformist and Hebrew (Volume 2).
Devon F.H.S. P.O. Box 9, Exeter EX2 6YP.
Webpage:
<www.devonfhs.org.uk/publications.htm>

Fursdon Index *(Devon and Cornwall Record Society)*, c/o West Country Studies Library, Exeter, EX4 3PQ. 25 parishes (mainly Exeter and environs), indexed in 9 vols. Also *Index of marriage licences 1523-1733* for the Diocese of Exeter. No postal enquiries. Index available only to members of *D&CRS.* Membership fees £16.50 per annum or £5 for temporary membership (3 months).

Boyd. In Main Series, 206 parishes, approx. 93% of county. All BTs from 1597-1673 are included. A copy of this index is in the possession of the *Devon and Cornwall Record Society.* No postal enquiries, conditions as Fursdon Index.

Pallot. 25 parishes.

DORSET

Published Registers. Many published parish registers are listed in S.A. Raymond, *Dorset: a genealogical bibliography.* FFHS, 1991.

Dorset Marriage Index *(Somerset and Dorset FHS).* Entries from original registers and Bishop's Transcripts, supplemented by printed transcripts and other printed sources. Alphabetically arranged, complete transcription of slip entries given. All parishes covered from commencement of surviving registers to 1837. Full list with periods covered, for £2.00 plus SAE (or 3 IRCs) Fees: £1 per specific marriage for members of the Somerset and Dorset FHS quoting membership number. £2 per marriage for non-members. Quotations given for one name block searches (for members only), on receipt of SAE. Sterling cheques only payable to *S & D FHS. Mr Ken and Mrs Val Andrew, 69 Sopwith Crescent, Merley, Wimborne, Dorset BH21 1SW.*
Webpage: **<www.sdfhs.org/Dormarr.htm>**
This database is also available online, pay-per-view, at:
<www.familyhistoryonline.net/database/ DorsetFHSmar.shtml>

Dorset continued

Marriage Licence Bonds for Sarum Diocese 1609-1837. (incl. Wiltshire, Berkshire and Dorset). Publication on CD from *Wiltshire FHS*, see page 29.

Dorset Online Parish Clerks have various transcripts of parish registers.
Webpage:
<www.dorset-opc.com/ChideockMarr.htm>

Boyd. In Miscellaneous Series. 79 parishes, approx. 27% of the county.

Pallot. 68 parishes.

Co. DURHAM

(Tyneside now in Tyne and Wear, Teeside now in Cleveland)

Durham County Council has an online index of civil registers held by district registrars.
Website:
<www.durham.gov.uk/DurhamCC/usp.nsf/pws/ Registrar+- +purchase+of+registration+certificates>

Gateshead Council also has an online index of civil registers held by district registrars.
<online.gateshead.gov.uk/bmd/>

Tees Valley Indexes. Online indexes to civil registers held by Middlesbrough, Hartlepool, Stockton-on-Tees and Redcar and Cleveland District Registrars.
Webpage: **<www.middlesbrough-indexes.co.uk/>**

Darlington Births Marriages and Deaths. Online index to civil registers.
<www.darlington.gov.uk/Living/ Register+Office/RegOfficeSearch.htm>

Northumberland and Durham Marriages *(Northumberland and Durham FHS)* This database contains 264,274 marriage entries from the registers of 124 parishes from the County Durham and 103 parishes from Northumberland.
Webpage: **<www.familyhistoryonline.net/ database/NDFHSmar.shtml>**

Co. Durham 1813-1837 *(Northumberland and Durham FHS).* Whole county, published on m'fche. Many indexed transcripts covering the whole of the county published on m'fche. List available.
N. & D. F.H.S., 2nd Floor, Bolbec Hall, Westgate Road, Newcastle upon Tyne NE1 1SE
Webpage:
<www.ndfhs.org.uk/Sales/index.html>

Co. Durham continued

Marriages Co. Durham. Durham 1798-1812, not in Boyd, Durham pre-1837 Non-Anglican Marriages, Auckland deanery Marriages 1813-1839, Barnard Castle Deanery 1813-1839, Brancepath 1840-1945 (Mrs I. Bowes), Chester-le-Street 1813-1839, Easington Deanery 1813-1839, Gateshead Deanery 1813-1839, Gateshead West Deanery 1813-1839, Hartlepool Deanery 1754-1812, and 1813-1839, Houghton-le-Spring Deanery 1813-1839, Jarrow 1813-1839, Lanchester Deanery 1813-1839, Sedgefield Deanery 1813-1839, Stanhope 1840-1901 (J.W.F. Rawling), Stockton 1813-1839, Sunderland July 1837-Oct 1846 (Mrs J.A. Lawrence). Publications on m'fche by George Bell and/or Carol Yellowley unless stated otherwise.

Also available on CD are Durham Marriages 1813-1837, Durham St Margaret 1558-1812 (Durham and Northumberland PRS), Durham St Nicholas 1540-1812, Ryton 1581-1812, Stanhope 1613-1812, Whickham 1579-1812 (all from DNPRS).

A series of Durham Marriage Bonds covering the years 1594-1812 are available on a set of 4 CDs indexed by George Bell. Pelton Holy Trinity Marriages 1843-1923 available as booklets.

These publications were originally issued by Original Indexes, but are now available from Ancestral Indexes eShop, which is run by Northumberland and Durham FHS.

Webpage:

North and Middle of the County. 88 parishes (161,800 marriages). Both parties, earliest date to 1837 in each parish. 70% orig. regs., 10% BTs, 20% printed sources. Complete date. Widows, lics. shown.

South Tyneside. 5 parishes up to turn of 20th century (19,000 marriages) + Jarrow St. Bede's R.C. April 1863-April 1916.

These indexes, compiled by the late W.E. Rounce, are now held by the N & D FHS, as above.

Marriages. Chester le Street 1582-1837, Ebenezer Methodist Church Roker Avenue 1912-1949, Gateshead 1608-1837, Herrington St Wesleyan Marriage Index 1902-1960, Sans St Marriage Index 1899-1963, So. Durham St. United Marriage Index 1900-1933, Holy Trinity East End Sunderland Marriage Index 1908-1987, Holy Trinity Church Marriage Index 4/7/1837-31/10/1846, Holy Trinity, Sunderland 1837-1846, Sunderland Marriages 1719-1837, Holy Trinity Sunderland Marriages 1846-1908, Houghton 1700-1837, St Michael Trimdon 1720-1837,West Rainton 1827-1837, Penshaw 1746-1837, South Shields, St Hildas, St Michaels. St. Michael, Bishopwearmouth 1568-1837. St Aidan, Grangetown Marriage Index 1911-1981 A-J, K-Z. St Andrew Deptford Baps and Marrs 1845-1851, St Mark Millfield Marriage Index 1872-1880, St Andrew Deptford 1845-1948. Ulgham Marriages, Newburn Marriages, St Andrew Marriages Bywell, Bothal, Wood Horn, Widdring, Croxdale, Bedlington,

Cramlington, Gainford, Ponteland, Warden, (dates not stated contact below for details), St Barnabas Hendon 1876-1967, St Barnabas 1876-1967, St Oswald 1943-1948, St Hilda Millfield 1894-1968, St. Peter's, Monkwearmouth 1837-1866, 1867-1909, 1911-1979, St Hilda South Shields 20/12/1653-17/6/1914, St Ignatius Hendon Sunderland 1889-1988,.St Ignatius Hendon Baps and Marrs 1889-1901, St John, East End 1875-1965, St Luke Pallion 1874-1911, St Cuthbert Monkwearmouth 1880-1939, St Marks Millfield 1881-1897. St Paul Hendon 1854-1969, St Peter Bishopwearmouth 1900-1948, Christ Church 1876-1901, St Thomas Bishopswearmouth Baps and Marrs 1862-1871, Marrs 1846-1943, Venerable Bede 1873-1890, Whitburn 1579-1837, Hebburn 1813-1839, Easington 1570-1837, Lambley 1747-1836, Bothal 1813-1837, Halton 1654-1769.

City Library and Arts Centre, Fawcett Street, Sunderland. SR1 1RE.

Durham Record Office Handlists.

Various marriage indexes are listed in the handlists which are kept updated online.
3. Modern Transcripts and Indexes (C of E).
6. Modern Transcripts and Indexes (Nonconformist).
7. Northumberland and North Yorkshire transcripts and Indexes (C of E).

County Archivist, Durham Record Office, County Hall, Durham DH1 5UL.
email: record.office@durham.gov.uk
Webpage: <www.durham.gov.uk/recordoffice/
usp.nsf/pws/durham+record+office+
-+durham+record+office+homepage>

West Durham Database. Covers one third of the county, west of Durham City from River Tyne to River Tees. Contains all baptisms, marriages and burials from the earliest dates up to December 1851.

Ron Nubley, 66 Alderside Crescent, Lanchester, Durham DH7 0PZ.

North Yorkshire and County Durham Marriages. At the moment this index includes Stockton 1707-51 only for Co. Durham; however, more is planned. Pay-per-view site.
<www.familyhistoryonline.net/database/
ClevelandFHSmar.shtml>

Boyd. In Main Series. 71 parishes, approx 69% of county. A copy of this index is deposited in Newcastle Public Library.

Joiner. 101 Co. Durham parishes; 182328 entries.

Pallot. 20 Parishes.

ESSEX

Published Registers. Many published parish registers are listed in S.A. Raymond, *Essex: the genealogist's library guide.* FFHS, 1998.

Essex. Mainly **1754-1851** (none later). Covers the ancient parishes of the county, including those now in Outer London area, plus one Quaker meeting. Augments Boyd, but has most Essex entries found in the Miscellaneous Series. Original registers used, with full details except names of witnesses and clergy, and (in most cases) the occupations of fathers in post Civil Registration registers. Male and female sections, arranged alphabetically, with many cross references to variants. Over 90% of the county with some cover but the 1837-51 period is less well served. For parishes whose registers are not yet deposited, BTs have been indexed separately (usually 1800-1837, with gaps). Please send full name of at least one partner, and an area of the county with which the family had known connections, if possible, and a 'not later than' year. Fees: U.K. SAE + £1 per marriage, Overseas US $2 (no return postage required) for a single marriage with $1.25 each for additional marriages up to $5, in the same letter.

Jack H. Baxter, 16 Chandos Parade, Benfleet, Essex SS7 2HT.

Essex Marriages in London 1675-1754. Males and females. Marriages in London and Middlesex of people from Essex parishes. Printed and original registers (including some Fleet marriages). Supplemented by Licences (London, Faculty Office and Vicar General). Nearly 6,000 marriages, full entry.

A. Benton, 46 Waldegrave Gardens, Upminster, Essex RM14 1UX.

Boyd. In main series, 381 parishes and one Meeting of Society of Friends. Approx. 94% of the county (much to 1754 or 1812 only). A copy of this index is at the *Essex Record Office.* Some parishes for 1801-1837 are in the Miscellaneous Series (not at Essex Record Office).

Pallot. 23 parishes.

Thames Riverside Parish Index. See under Kent, page 16.

Catholic Marriage Index, 1837-1870. See entry under London and Middlesex, page 21.

Marriage Licences. Held by *ERO Chelmsford* which has a (nearly complete) manuscript index. A separate index covers the Peculiars. An index held by *Colchester Local Studies Library.* The *Society of Genealogists* has a number of Essex marriage license indexes.

Canterbury Peculiars Marriage Licence Index.
A surname index to the marriage licences issued in various peculiars which came under the jurisdiction of the Archbishop of Canterbury. These peculiars included the Deanery of Bocking (Essex), Lambeth Palace Library have completed the index for Bocking.

GLOUCESTERSHIRE and BRISTOL

Published Registers and Indexes. Many published registers are listed in S.A. Raymond, *Gloucestershire and Bristol: a genealogical bibliography.* FFHS, 1992.

Gloucestershire 1800-37. On m'fche.
West Glamorgan Archives Service, County Hall, Swansea.
Webpage:
<**www.swansea.gov.uk/westglamorganarchives**>

Gloucestershire Marriage Index, 1800-1837 *(Gloucestershire FHS).* Now complete for Gloucester **Diocese**, 70,000 marriages 1800-1837. Search fee, one surname, no variants £2.00 (payable to GFHS) plus SAE or 2 IRCs. Includes up to one A4 print out. Also published on CD and is available from the society. Check the web site for details of purchase.
Mrs. Janet Selley, Penlea, Selsley West, Stroud, Glos. GL5 5LJ.
Webpage: <**www.gfhs.org.uk**>

Boyd. In Main Series. 200 parishes, from Phillimore printed registers including extracts from Bristol and Gloucestershire Marriage Licences and Bonds and refs. to Glos. in Phillimore Wiltshire registers. This county was indexed by the late E.A. Roe and typed by the Church of Latter Day Saints. Boyd's index was continued by Roe, and the joint coverage is listed in the *Guide to Boyd's Marriage Index.* For the post-1800 period, 33% of the county is covered to 1837 and 20% to 1812. Copies are held by the *Society of Genealogists* and by *Gloucestershire Record Office, Gloucester GL1 2HY.*

Pallot. 124 parishes.

Bristol Marriages 1800-1837. *(Bristol and Avon FHS).* On m'fche: Vols.1-7. New Bristol Marriages 1837-1885, St. James Barton and St. Paul's Portland Square Volumes available at *Bristol Record Office.*
On CD: Marriage Index Vol.8. Diocese of Bristol 1813-1837. Volume 10. North Somerset Parishes, 1754-1837.
Diane Pearce, 3, Elm Tree Park, Sheepway, Portbury, Bristol BS20 7WW.
Webpage:
<**www.bafhs.org.uk/shop/marriages.htm**>

The Marriage Index for Bristol and Avon 1754 - 1837. The Society has made indexes of marriages for all parishes in Bristol and Avon, 1754 - 1837, with some earlier. Although some of these are available on M'fiche and CD (as above), checks can be still be made against the original index. Normal charge £2 for each individual marriage.
Mrs Janet Hiscocks, "Beanacre", Easter Compton, Bristol, BS35 5RJ.
Webpage:
<**www.bafhs.org.uk/services/marriageindex.htm**>

GREATER MANCHESTER
See Lancashire.

HAMPSHIRE and the ISLE OF WIGHT
(Isle of Wight now a separate county)

Published Registers. A full list of published registers is provided by S.A. Raymond, *Hampshire: a genealogical bibliography.* FFHS, 1995.

The **Parish Register Transcription Society** has transcribed many Hampshire parish registers, which are now available on CD.
Website:

Hampshire Genealogical Society Marriage Index 1538-1837. Computerised, searchable both parties. Year only. Fees, individual entry £1.50 + SAE. Blanket search, send SAE or email for quotation. Charged at 5p per entry found, minimum fee £3, to a maximum of £20 SAE or email for results.
Rose Conway, 18 Waterbeech Drive, Hedge End, Southampton SO30 4NJ.
email: *rose.conway@zetnet.co.uk*
Webpage: **<hgs-online.org.uk/research.htm>**

Marriage Indexes to the majority of pre 1900 marriages are available in the Searchroom. The project is ongoing.
Portsmouth City Museum and Records Office, Museum Road, Portsmouth PO1 2LJ.
email: *Searchroom@portsmouthcc.gov.uk*
A number of **Quaker Marriages in Hampshire 1663-1837** are indexed online at:
<webpage.lineone.net/~hantshistory/mm.html>

Isle of Wight

Isle of Wight Marriage Index 1837-2000. Searchable database from information provided by the IOW Register Office.
Webpage:

Isle of Wight Marriage Index 1539-1837. Complete, both parties, from orig. regs. Some with complete dates, others year only. Widows shown. Phonetic. This is part of an extensive card index to transcribed entries from baptism, marriage and burial registers. Additional card index **1838-1899**, m'fiche index **1900-1910**. No fee for visitors to the Record Office but a fee is payable for postal searches.
County Archivist, Isle of Wight R.O., 26 Hillside, Newport, Isle of Wight.
Webpage:
<www.iwight.com/library/record_office/default.asp>

Edwardian Marriage Index *(Isle of Wight FHS)* Lists all 3,500 Anglican and Roman Catholic Marriages from 1901-1910, alphabetically sorted by groom and bride, together with fathers. Published on 2 m'fiche. price £3.00, pandp 50p UK £1.00 anywhere airmail. If more than 1 fiche item ordered, only one pandp payable. Cash with orders please, all cheques in sterling to:
Mr Barry. Hall, Woodmoor, 1A Hungerberry Close, Shanklin, Isle of Wight, PO37 6LX
email: *bhalliow@aol.com.*

Victorian Marriage Index 1837-1900 *(Isle of Wight FHS).* Lists all 18,540 Anglican and Roman Catholic Marriages from 1837-1900, alphabetically sorted by groom and bride, together with fathers, parish by parish. Published on 12 m'fiche £20.00 pandp 50p UK, £1.00 anywhere airmail. Details as left.

Victorian Marriage Index available on CD, 1837-31st December 1900. Published in a continuous sort for Bride and Groom for ALL Anglican and R.C. Marriages plus all Register Office and Authorised Persons Marriages for the same period, covering every marriage on the Isle of Wight. Facility to print out hard copies of all surnames being researched. £20 + £1 p&p.
Mr. Barry Hall, as left.
Webpage:
(click on 'Publications' and 'Indexes published by Barry Hall')

Boyd. In Miscellaneous Series. 107 parishes approx. 35% of mainland county, plus Isle of Wight, 28 parishes (90% of the island).

Pallot. 115 parishes.

HEREFORDSHIRE

Herefordshire Marriage Index 1538-1837 *(Herefordshire FHS).* 112,062 marriage entries from parish registers in Herefordshire Record Office; also including some strays. Online index; pay-per-view.
<www.familyhistoryonline.net/database/HerefsFHSmar.shtml>

Herefordshire and part of **Radnorshire** (within Hereford Diocese), **1538-1754** *(Herefordshire FHS).* Both parties (from PRs and BTs), plus many strays. SAE + £1 for one entry to £20 per 100. Bulk extraction by negotiation.
Mr J. Harnden, 11 Longworth Road, Tupsley, Hereford HR1 1SP.

1754-1837. Both parties (PRs and BTs). Strays from surrounding counties are incl.. Terms as above.
Mrs V. Hadley, 255 Whitecross Rd, Hereford HR4 0LT.

Herefordshire Parish Register *(Powys FHS).* M'fiche or booklet. Transcripts of Baps, Banns, Marriages & Burials 1681-1901 (in Adobe pdf. format on CD).
Winforton 1691-1900 (incl. 1841-1871 census).
Mr Mike MacSorley, 20 Hospital Road, Penpedairheol, Hengoed, Mid-Glam, CF82 8DG
email: *m.macsorley@btopenworld.com*
Also available at **<www.parishchest.co.uk>**
(click on 'Family History Societies' and 'Powys FHS')

Herefordshire 1660-1837. Males only. Whole county incl. some Welsh border parishes. In progress. From BTs. No printed sources used. Complete date. Widows shown. Alphabetical. Similar names supplied. Pub'd on m'fiche 1701-1837.
Mr Bertram Merrell, 3912 South 2520 West, West Valley City, Utah 84119, USA.

Boyd. In Miscellaneous Series. Six parishes only.
Pallot. 11 parishes.

HERTFORDSHIRE

The Allen Index. Both parties to 1837. Covers all parishes in the county, 25% from printed sources. Year only. Widows shown. Arranged by Allen's own standardised spellings alphabetically, with cross references. Most of the index now available on searchable database.
Hertfordshire Archives and Local Studies, County Hall, Pegs Lane, Hertford, Herts. SG13 8EJ.
email: *herts.direct@hertscc.gov.uk*
Webpage: **<www.hertsdirect.org/hals>**

Fleet Marriages of Hertfordshire People to 1754. Book or m'fche *(Publication from Hertfordshire FHS).* Further details from:
Booksales Officer, Hertfordshire FHS, 24 Ashurst Road, Barnet EN4 9LF
email: *postsales@hertfhs.org.uk*
Webpage: **<www.hertsfhs.org.uk/hfphs6.html>**

Boyd. In Miscellaneous Series. 48 parishes, approx. 36% of the county.

Joiner. 131 parishes; 106563 entries.

Pallot. 35 parishes.

HUNTINGDONSHIRE
(now part of Cambridgeshire)

Huntingdonshire Marriage Index 1601-1754. Typescript index, compiled by Marian Green, Jean Pothecary and others; covers entire ancient county. **1754-1837** compiled by T.P.R. Laing; covers ancient county and Thorney (Cambs). Both indexes are both parties, original registers supplemented by BTs, year only, widows shown.
County Record Office, Grammar School Walk, Huntingdon PE18 6LF.
Webpage: **<www.cambridgeshire.gov.uk/ leisure/archives/visiting/crohuntingdon.htm>**

Marriage Allegations and Bonds index 1663-1883 for the Archdeaconry of Huntingdon, on cards, one party only listed. No fees. Copies also at *CRO Cambridge* and *Peterborough Central Library*.
County Record Office, Huntingdon, as above.

Huntingdonshire Marriage Index 1601-1700, 1701-1754, and 1754-1837. Publications on m'fche from *Huntingdonshire FHS.*
HFHS Publications, 42 Crowhill, Godmanchester, Huntingdon Cambs PE29 2NR.
email: *bookstall@huntsfhs.org.uk*
Webpage: **<www.huntsfhs.org.uk/Pubs.html>**

Boyd. In Miscellaneous Series. 17 parishes (approx. 16% of the county).

KENT

Published Registers. A full listing of published registers is provided by S.A. Raymond, *Kent: a genealogical bibliography, vol.2: registers, inscriptions, and wills.* FFHS, 1998.

Kent FHS Publications. Many parish registers transcribed. Visit the webpage, or obtain a full list of m'fche publications (price £2.00 + 47p p&p members and £3.00 + postage to non-members).
Mrs R.J. Bailey, 41 The Street, Kennington, Ashford, Kent TN24 9HD.
Webpage: **<www.kfhs.org.uk/>**

Kent 1813-1837. Complete for available material. Both parties. From printed sources and TS copies; some from BTs. Complete date and marital status given. Phonetic arrangement. Similar names supplied. Fee £6 minimum.
M.J. Gandy, 3 Church Crescent, Whetstone, London N20 0JR.
email: *mgandy@clara.co.uk*

Eastern Kent 1754-1812. Complete for available material. Details as above. List of parishes available. Fee £6 minimum. *M.J. Gandy, as above.*

East Kent 1538-1639, 1640-1660, 1661-1699 and 1700-1753 all parishes covered. Indexed by groom's name for earlier periods and by both groom and bride for 1700-1753. £5 + SAE for individual marriage, £10 + SAE for up to 25 refs. to a single surname. Estimates for blanket extractions given on receipt of details of surname and period required and SAE.
Mrs J. Jones, Weir Bank Lodge, Monkey Island Lane, Bray, Maidenhead, Berks. SL6 2ED.

West Kent 1538-1812. All the Rochester Diocese, and Shoreham Deanery, incl. parishes in South East London. The index now has **complete coverage** with c.160,000 marriages. Males only indexed. orig. regs. Complete date, widows, abode, lics., shown. Arranged phonetically. Parish list sent with each enquiry. Fee £6 minimum per search. List of entries for the same surname, an additional 50p per entry.
S.G. Smith, 59 Friar Rd, Orpington, Kent BR5 2BW.
email: *sydney.smith7@ntlworld.com*

Folkestone SS Mary and Eanswythe, 1635-1866 (typed transcripts + index).
Lyminge SS Mary and Ethelburga 1538-1837 (typed transcripts + index).
Folkestone Library.

Thames Riverside Parish Series. Nearly all of North West Kent riverside parishes now covered, with some for Essex and Surrey now available.) Full details on webpage.
R.J. Cottrell, 19 Bellevue Road, Bexleyheath, Kent DA6 8ND.
email: *RJCindex@aol.com.*
Webpage:
<hometown.aol.com/rjcindex/trueflare.html>

Kent *continued*

Selon Index: Kent parishes in S.E. London. Deptford 1754-84, Charlton 1653-1809, Woolwich 1746-54 from orig. regs. List Available. Fee £5 minimum. *Peter R. Shilham, 6 Beckford Close, Wokingham, Berks. RG41 1HN.*

Rochester Archdeaconry area Parish Registers. Baptisms, marriages and burials 16-20th c. (MF); Rochester Cathedral births 1657-1757, baptisms 1657-1994, **marriages 1669-1754**, and burials 1633-1890 (DRc; MFs 273, 421). **Many digitised images of parish registers are online.**
NonConformist Records – Medway Area. Microfilm of Nonconformist registers, Medway area 1700-1837, originals held at *The National Archives*, MF 160.
Ecclesiastical
Records of the Cathedral Priory of St. Andrew the Apostle, Rochester [604] c.1080-1541.
Records of the Cathedral Church of Christ and the Blessed Virgin Mary Rochester 1541-1994.
Medway Archives and Local Studies Centre, Civic Centre, Strood, Kent, ME2 4AU
email: *local.studies@medway.gov.uk*
webpage:
<cityark.medway.gov.uk/about/localstudies>

Kent Baptisms Marriages and Burials. A database of slected entries is provided at **<www.rootsweb.com/~engken/bmd.html>**

Canterbury Peculiars Marriage Licence Index. A surname index to the marriage licences issued in various peculiars which came under the jurisdiction of the Archbishop of Canterbury. These peculiars included the Deanery of Shoreham (Kent)

Boyd. In Miscellaneous Series. 130 parishes (approx 32% of county) but mostly 1661-75 and 1701-25 only.

Pallot. 30 parishes.

LANCASHIRE
(now partly in Greater Manchester, Merseyside and Cumbria)

Published Registers. Numerous published registers and indexes are listed in S.A. Raymond, *Lancashire: a genealogical bibliography. Vol 2. Registers Inscriptions and wills.* FFHS, 1996.

Many parish registers have been transcribed, indexed, and published by the *Lancashire Parish Register Society.*
Webpage:
<www.genuki.org.uk/big/eng/LAN/lprs/>

Lancashire BMD: Births, Marriages and Deaths on the Internet. Index to civil registers held by RDs, 1837-present day, but not yet complete.
Webpage:
<www.lancashirebmd.org.uk>

Lancashire *continued*

Lancashire Marriage Index. *(Lancashire Family History and Heraldry Society).* **1813-1837** except those shown. Parishes not in Boyd. Both parties. Covers Accrington (St. James), Ainsworth 1812-37, Altcar 1800-58, Altham, Ashworth (Middleton) 1824-40, Billinge 1813-26, 1830-36 (from BTs), Blackburn St Joseph R.C. (Audley) 1874-1917,1917-1931, 1931-1989, Blackburn St. Mary the Virgin 1680-1721, 1722-1754, Blackburn Pleasington Priory St Mary and St John the Baptist (RC) 2. 1854-3, 1982, Blackburn St Peter's in Chains R.C. 1934-1999, Bolton by Bowland, Bolton le Moors St. Peter, Brindle St. Joseph (RC) 1834-1934, Burnley St. Peter, Bury St. Mary 1800-09, 1810-19, 1820-29, and 1830-37, Charnock Richard (Chorley) Christ Church 1860-1953, Chorley St. Lawrence 1837-1900, Church and Church Kirk, Clitheroe, St Mary Magdalene, Colne, Croston chapelry of Becconsall 1813-46, Croston chapelry of Bretherton 1843-46, Croston chapelry of Mawdsley 1843-46, Deane (Bolton), Downham, Eccles, Edenfield parish church 1837-2000, Elswick United Reform church Feb 1912-1993, Gisburn St. Mary the Virgin (Yorks) 1813-1837, 1837-1893, Great Ecclestone Copp St. Anne's (complete register), Great Ecclestone St. Mary's RC (whole reg), Great Harwood, Halsall Parish Church 1812-37 Halton, (Lancaster), Haslingden St. James, Hesketh with Becconsall 1823-1829, Hollinwood St. Margaret 1836-43, Long Preston Baptist Church 1854-1957, Lytham St. Peter (RC) 1837-1940, Mawdesley 1871-83, Melling, Middleton 1805-1837, Mid Marton (Blackpool) 1838-1900, Newchurch in Pendle, Newchurch in Rossendale, Oldham Bardsley PC, Oldham Greenacres Independent Chapel 1850-1890, Oldham Independant Methodist, George Street, 1927-1986, Oldham St. Mary, Padiham, Overton St. Helen, Penwortham, Radcliffe St. Mary 1810-1837, Rochdale St. Chad and Wardleworth chapelry, Rochdale Hope Chapel 1844-1926, Saddleworth St. Chad 1800-37, Spotland (Rochdale) St Clement 1837-1990, St. Helen's Prescot parish, Tatham, Up Holland, Walton-le-Dale St Leonard 1813-1837, Whalley 60% from orig. regs., 15% from BTs, 25% from printed sources. Year only. Alphabetical. Widows not shown. Further ongoing projects are Bury Bethel Independent Chapel Marriages 1876-1924 (also Baps & Burs) and Preesall Bethel United Reformed Church 1879-2001. This is not an integral index, please indicate which parishes you would like the search to cover. Donations (minimum £1) to be commensurate with the amount of work involved, Block searches for one surname with prior consultation. Requests (with donations and SAE please) to:
Thelma Simpson, 45 Leyster Street, Morecambe, Lancs, LA4 6HQ.
M'fiche purchases: *Mrs Dorothy Haworth, 24 Cecil Street, Oswaldtwistle, Lancs BB5 3HF*
Webpage:
<www.lfhhs.org.uk/shop/fiche/index.htm>

Marriage Indexes. St Mary's Todmorden 1st Jan 1807- 30th June 1837 in book form. Transcribed from original registers. Prestwich Marriages 1754-1800 (7 fiche), transcripts of the marriage register with full index to brides and grooms. Stockport Marriages 1799-1837 (4 fiche) arranged by male surname with index to females. Marriages Bolton Parish Church 1661-1712 (1 fiche), Marriage Bolton Parish Church 1713-1753 (6 fiche), 1754-1800 (3 fiche), 1800-1812 Index and part transcription (5 fiche) 1838-1850 (4 fiche), Marriages St Mary's Deane 1813-1854 (5 fiche). Mail order catalogue available from: *Manchester and Lancashire FHS, Clayton House, 59 Piccadilly, Manchester M1 2AQ.* Webpage: <**www.mlfhs.org.uk/Bookshop/index.html**>

Marriage Indexes. Crawshawbooth St John the Evangelist 1900-2002, Edenfield Parish Church Bride Index 1837-1907 (book and m'fche), Edgeside Mount Zion Baptist Church 1909-1999, Haslingden St. James C.E Marriage Index 1813-1837 (m'fche), Haslingden New Jerusalem Church 1843-1989, Newchurch St. Nicholas C.E. Marriage Index 1813-1837 (m'fche), Goodshaw Baptist Chapel Marriage Index 1862-1881 (book), St Mary and All Saints, Goodshaw 1907-1991, Newchurch Bethlehem Unitarian Church 1863-1907, Rawtenstall Unitarian Church Marriage Index 1866-1959, Stonefold St John's 1890-1947, Waterfoot Bethel Baptist Church Marriage Index 1915-1993 (book).
Rawtenstall Reference and Local Studies Library
email: *Rawtenstall.Reference@lcl.lancscc.goc.uk*

North Lancashire and Westmorland 1700-1837. Covers the whole of Westmorland and the Furness and Cartmel area of Lancs. (now in Cumbria) Males only indexed, over *c.*40,000 marriages. 1813-1837 complete coverage, earlier period *c.*80% coverage; Complete date, widows shown and whether by Lic. Arranged phonetically. Parish list with each enquiry.
S.G. Smith, 59 Friar Road, Orpington, Kent BR5 2BW.

N.E. Lancs. and Yorkshire Border Marriage Index 1700-1837 (but many to 1812 only, to avoid duplication with Lancashire FHS index). The ancient parish of Whalley with its chapelries, and parishes northwards towards Westmorland (incl. Accrington, Altham, Barnoldswick, Blackpool, Bolton by Bowland, Bracewell, Church, Clitheroe, Dent, Downham, Garsdale, Gisburn, Halton, Haslingden, Holme in Cliviger, Mitton, Newchurch in Rossendale, Overton, Padiham, Poulton le Sands, Sedbergh, Slaidburn, Warton, Waddington, Whalley and Whitewell). Mainly original registers (60%). Complete date. Widows shown. Alphabetical. 20,000 entries. List of parishes supplied. Fee £2 per marriage + SAE. Lists of one surname by arrangement.
Mrs B.H. Smith, The Shieling, Old Back Lane, Wiswell, Clitheroe, Lancs. BB7 9BS.

Liverpool & SW Lancs FHS. M'fche publications Altcar (Bishops Transcripts) Marriage Index 1800-1858 (Fiche 1);
Billinge Marriage Index 1813-1826/1830-36 (extracted from the Bishops Transcripts) (Fiche 1)
Liverpool St. Peter; Index of Marriages 1800-1837(Fiche 6);
Melling Marriage Index 1813-1837(Fiche 7);
St. Helens (Prescot Parish); Marriage Index 1813-1837(Fiche 9);
Upholland (BTs); Marriage Index 1813-37(Fiche 10);
Mr Joe Griffiths, 9 Manor Road, Lymm, Cheshire WA13 0AY.
email: *publications@liverpool-genealogy.org.uk*
Webpage:
<**www.liverpool-genealogy.org.uk/home.htm**>

Barrow in Furness St. George 1861-1880. 3 card index drawers in searchroom.
Cumbria Record Office and Local Studies Library, Barrow Branch, 140 Duke Street, Barrow in Furness LA14 1XW.
email: *barrow.record.office@cumbriacc.gov.uk*

Bickerstaffe Quakers 1650-1800 Births, Marriages and Burials *(Ormskirk and District FHS),* publication in books form. *PO Box 213, Aughton, Ormskirk, Lancashire L39 5WT.*
webpage: <**www.odfhs.org.uk/**>
email: *secretary@odfhs.org.uk*

St. Mary's Church, Kirkdale, Liverpool: 4th October 1874 to 11th December 1883. An online index to the Marriages extracted from LDS film #1545938, containing all the names of the Brides and Grooms.
Tom Miller, 1266 Pallatine Drive, Oakville, Ontario, L6H 1Z2, Canada.
Webpage: <**www.genuki.org.uk/big/eng/LAN/ Liverpool/St.Mary-marr-1874-1883.txt**>

Liverpool Marriages *(Liverpool and SW Lancs FHS).* The St. Peter's Church Parish Registers of Marriages contain 19,264 records for the period January 1800 to June 1837. The registers of St Anne's, Richmond contain 9,543 marriages between 1773 and 1837.
<**www.familyhistoryonline.net/database/ SWLancsFHSmar.shtml**>

Manchester and Lancs. FHS. Microfiche publications of parish registers (especially Oldham area). Send SAE for price list to:
The Bookshop, Manchester and Lancs FHS, Clayton House, 59 Piccadilly, Manchester M1 2AQ.
Webpage:
<**www.mlfhs.org.uk/Bookshop/index.html**>

Warrington Marriage Index prior to Civil Registration. *(Liverpool and S.W. Lancs. FHS). (Warrington Group).* The index contains 26,531 entries. Each contains the following. Name of groom, and bride (indexed separately), occupation (if stated), place and/or parish of residence (if stated), name of church, whether by banns or licence, date of marriage, names of witnesses. The index contains details from the following churches, Burtonwood, St. Michael and All Angels 1683-1750 inclusive, Culcheth, Newchurch parish church 1607-1751 incl, Grappenhall, St. Wilfrid 1574-1837 incl, Great Sankey, St. Mary 1730-1752 incl, Hollinfare, St. Helen 1705-1837 incl, Latchford St. James 1833-1837incl, Lymm, St. Mary the Virgin 1568-1837incl, Warrington, St. Elphin 1707-1837 incl. Warrington, St. Paul April 1837-July 1837. The cost for a search is £1 per marriage, dollar bills or sterling money orders only from outside UK. Please make out to: *D. Forrest, 83 Wash Lane, Warrington WA4 1JD.*

Marriage Indexes, Wigan Area
1. Abram St John CE 1854-1966,
2. Billinge St Aidan CE 1699-1989, also fiche 1813-1826,1830-36.
3. Christ Church CE Charnock Richard 1860-1900.
4. Chorley St Lawrence CE 1837-1900.
5. Ince St Mary CE 1888-1976.
6. Pemberton St John CE 1835-1926.
7. Shevington St Anne CE 1887-1928.
8. Skelmersdale St Paul CE 1859-1980 (fiche).
9. Upholland St Thomas CE 1837-2004 (also Bishop Transcripts 1813-37 (fiche)).
10. Wigan Queen's Hall Wesleyan Methodist Mission 1945-1968.
11. Prescot St Helen CE 1813-37 (fiche).
12. Boyd's Marriage Index for Lancashire (fiche).
Wigan Heritage Services, The History Shop, Library St., WN1 1NU.
email: *heritage@wict.org*
Website:
<www.wlct.org/Culture/Heritage/fhistory.htm>

Boyd. In Main Series. 102 parishes. Approx. 31% of the county.

Pallot. 14 parishes.

LEICESTERSHIRE

Leicestershire Marriage Index 1801-1837. Complete, does not include Rutland (see page 24), both parties, year only. Original registers and BTs used for each parish where possible. No fee for single entry, donations welcome.

1754-1800. Leicester parishes indexed. The County's western half should also now have been completed.
Mr R.E. Makins, 45 Westcotes Drive, Leicester LE3 0QT.

Leicestershire Parish Register indexes. *(Leicestershire and Rutland FHS).* CD containing transcriptions of christenings, burials and marriages in 66 parishes of Leicestershire, and comes with it's own fully searchable database software. It contains over 300,000 entries, giving a total of over 1 million names from the start of parish registers up to, in some cases, the 1900s. This is the first disc of an on-going project. For full details of the parishes contained on the CD, go to
<www.lrfhs.net/parishindex>
LRFHS Bookshop, 101 High Street, Leicester LE1 4JB
Webpage: <www.lrfhs.net/onlinesales.htm>

Leicestershire and Rutland Stray Marriages. *(Leicestershire and Rutland FHS).* This index consists of 13,102 entries. Pay per-view website.
<www.familyhistoryonline.net/database LEIStrayMarriages.shtml>

Leicester Marriage Index 1801-37 (The Borough) Surnames A-E
Leicester Marriage Index 1801-37 (The Borough)Surnames F-K
Leicester Marriage Index 1801-37 (The Borough)Surnames L-R
Leicester Marriage Index 1801-37 (The Borough)Surnames S-Z
Leicestershire Marriage Index 1538-1754, Part 1
Above volume covers Bitteswell, Claybrooke and Lutterworth only
Leicestershire Marriage Index 1700-1753 Part 2
Above volume covers Ashby De La Zouch, Belton, Blackfordby, Breedon On The Hill, Castle Donington, Coleorton, Diseworth, Isley Walton, Lockington, Netherseal, Normanton Le Heath, Osgathorpe, Packington and Whitwick.
See *LRFHS Bookshop*, as above.

Leicester Marriages *(Leicestershire and Rutland FHS).* Over 6,600 marriages. Pay-per-view website.
<www.familyhistoryonline.net/database/ LRFHSmar.shtml>

Phillimores Leicestershire marriages. CD from *LRFHS* bookshop as above. For details of parishes covered, see
webpage: <www.lrfhs.net/phillimores>

Marriage Bonds for the Archdeaconry of Leicester 1570-1891.
Peculiars of Leicester St Margaret 1672-1720, 1724-1880, Rothley Peculiar 1682-1695, 1735-1857, Evington Peculiar 1632-1848.
The bonds are indexed in H. Hartopp, ed. *Leicestershire Marriage Licenses 1570-1729* (BRS: Index Library 38), which is also available on *Ancestry.com* CD English Parish Records: Lincs., Leics. and Rutland and in a card index for 1730-1891.

Leicestershire continued

Marriage Registers. Leicester and Leicestershire (CD and vols), whole county. *(All compiled by Leicestershire and Rutland FHS)* Leicester 1754-1800 (CD), Rutland (whole county) 1754-1837 (volumes), 67 Leicestershire parishes $16^{th}-20^{th}$c. (CD: The Leicester Project parish index and viewer). 43 Leicestershire and Rutland Parishes $16^{th}-19^{th}$c (*Ancestry.com* CD as above).
14 Parishes in N.W. Leics 1538-1753 (2 vols, comp S. Brown). Bitteswell, Claybrooke and Lutterworth 1538-1754 (Leics Marriage Index Vol.1). 14 Parishes in N.W,Leics 1700-1753 (Leics Marriage Index Vol.11). Strays Marriage Index: over 13,000 marriages of couples who "strayed" out of Leic and Rutland. CD). Leicester St Margaret 1837-1897 (CD).
Webpage: <**lrfhs.org.uk/publications.html**>

Marriage Announcements in *Leicester Chronicle* and *Leicester Journal* c.1799-1833 (card index)
The Record Office for Leicestershire, Leicester and Rutland, Wigston Magna, Leicester LE18 2AH.
Webpage: <**www.leics.gov.uk/index/ community/museums/record_office.htm**>

Boyd. In Miscellaneous Series. 140 parishes, approx. 51% of county, but many 1651-1675, 1701-1725 only.
Joiner. 57 parishes; 22,681 entries.
Pallot. 102 parishes.

LINCOLNSHIRE

Published Registers. A full list of published registers and indexes is provided by Raymond, S.A. *Lincolnshire: a genealogical bibliography.* FFHS, 1995.

Lincolnshire Marriage Index, 1754-1812, 1813-1837 published in A5 format booklets.
Boston St. Botolph Marriages 1813-37 published on m'fche.
Great Grimsby area Marriages 1844-1879 (mostly nonconformist) on m'fche.
1657-1853 Quaker and other nonconformist marriages (incs Lincs Quaker Digest; Gen Baptist Church Killingholme; Boston St Mary, Irnham/Corby Glen and St Hugh Lincoln Roman Catholic; Wesleyan Methodist register for Saltfleet 1770-1800, births, marriages and deaths). Full publication and price list available from:
The Postal Sales Officer, Unit 6, 33 Monks Ways, Monks Road, Lincoln LN2 5LN.
Webpage: <**www.lincolnshirefhs.org.uk**>

Lincolnshire Marriage Bonds and Allegations. Database of 17,978 bonds and allegations, with 35,956 entries, covering 1628-1811. Pay per view.
Webpage: <**www.familyhistoryonline.net/ database/LincolnshireFHSmlb.shtml**>

Boyd. In Miscellaneous Series. 99 parishes (approx. 15% of county), mostly short periods.
Joiner. 77 parishes; 52652 entries.
Pallot. 72 parishes.

LONDON and MIDDLESEX

Note: For marriage indexes, which generally relate to pre-1837 years, areas now thought of as London' will be found not only in Middlesex, but also in Essex, Kent and Surrey (Southwark in particular). By the time of the censuses, 1841-1891, London was established as a metropolitan area, and so the same areas are more likely to be classified as London than in their original counties. Nevertheless it is always wise to check under both London and under the individual counties of Essex, Kent and Surrey as appropriate.

Tower Hamlets Births, Deaths and Marriages. Index to civil registers held by district registrars.
Webpage: <**www.thbmd.co.uk/**>

Indexes held by Members (of W.Midd'x FHS) (including some listed separately below) are listed on their webpage:
<**www.west-middlesex-fhs.org.uk/ wmfhsind.html**>

Published registers. Many published parish registers, marriage licences, indexes, etc., are listed in S.A. Raymond, *London and Middlesex: a genealogical bibliography. Vol.1. Genealogical sources.* 2nd ed. FFHS., 1998. This listing includes many publications of the Harleian Society, as well as Phillimore registers, *etc.*

Middlesex Parish Records. Index to Phillimore parish register series for Middlesex.
Webpage:
<**www.angelfire.com/fl/Sumter/Middlesex.html**>

Boyd. In Main and Miscellaneous Series, 177 parishes etc., some extracts only, incl. some London Marriage Licences and many Hugenot Registers. Approx. 73% of the city and county. A copy of the index is at the Guildhall Library.
Webpage (for details of Guildhall Library copy):
<**www.cityoflondon.gov.uk/Corporation/ leisure_heritage/libraries_archives_museums_ galleries/city_london_libraries/guildhall+library +guides.htm**> (click on 'Boyd's Marriage Index')

Pallot. One of the most important and useful indexes of marriages. For those whose ancestry is lost in London before General Registration this is an essential source. It covers all but two of the 103 ancient parishes of the old City of London for the period 1780-1837 – with entries taken from original sources, many now lost. The index has been augmented by entries from other countries, usually transcribed from printed sources. There was an equivalent baptismal section but this was severely damaged during World War II; however, some 100,000 entries survive. A catalogue is available for £5.00. A CD of the Index is available. Searches are carried out at the library search rate.
Institute of Heraldic and Genealogical Studies, Northgate, Canterbury, Kent CT1 1BA
Webpage: <**www.ihgs.ac.uk**>

London and Middlesex *continued*

`Catholic Marriage Index, 1837-1870.` Covers 60 parishes in London (north of the Thames) and Essex. A list of the coverage of parishes in Central London only is available, along with a more detailed leaflet describing this collection. Searches are carried out at the library search rate. Now available on m'fche.
Institute of Heraldic and Genealogical Studies, as page 20, left.

Crisp's London Marriage Licences Index. An index to some original marriage licences of over a dozen major London parishes is held. These include St. Martin in the Fields 1765-1837; St. Mary, Putney 1822-1837; Holy Trinity, Chelsea 1832-1837; St. Leonard, Shoreditch 1774-1837; St. Dunstan in the West 1731-1837; St. Paul, Deptford 1779-1833; Christ Church, Spittlefields 1757-1780; St. John, Hackney 1779-1837; St. Paul, Covent Garden 1734-1837; Kensington, Deptford, Whitechapel (some) etc., 1707-1837. All are abstracted and indexed and in many cases the original licences are also held. Searches are carried out at the library search rate. A free surname only index is available online at:
<www.achievements.co.uk/services/ londonmarriage/index.php>
Institute of Heraldic and Genealogical Studies, as page 20, left.

Marriage Licence Records (Allegations and Bonds) at Guildhall Library. For details of indexes etc, visit the webpage:
<www.history.ac.uk/gh/marrlic.htm>

For details of some **marriage licence indexes available on CD**, visit:
<www.rod-neep.co.uk/acatalog/ eng-marriagelic.html>

Selon Index (mainly S.E. London) 20 parishes, 16 from Phillimore. Mainly one party only for the Middlesex Phillimore marriage index, parties to 1812 or 1837. All from copies, but already in Boyd. List available. Minimum fee £5.00.
Peter Shilham, 6 Beckford Close, Wokingham, Berks. RG41 1HN.

Canterbury Peculiars Marriage Licence Index. A surname index to the marriage licences issued in various peculiars which came under the jurisdiction of the Archbishop of Canterbury. These peculiars included the Deanery of the Arches (London) and Croydon (Surrey and Middlesex). *Lambeth Palace Library* have completed the index for Bocking (Essex).

Fleet Marriages found in St. Martin's in the Fields Settlement Examinations 1732-1795.
Webpage: **<www.westminster.gov.uk/libraries/ archives/indexes/sett_intro.cfm>**

Fleet Marriages 1690-1754 Ongoing project by:
City of Westminster Archives Centre, 10 St. Ann's Street, London SW1P 2XR.
webpage: **<www.westminster.gov.uk/archives>**

Middlesex (only)

West Middlesex Marriage Index. *(West Middx. FHS).* About 85,000 pre-1837 marriages in West Middlesex with partial coverage elsewhere in the county. Search for one specific marriage reference £1.00 (non members £2.00); listing of up to 20 entries for specific surname £2.00 (non members £4.00). Please supply places/dates/surname variants if known. All enquiries must contain SAE (minimum 220x110mm). Cheques payable to West Middlesex FHS).
Richard Chapman, 15 Willerton Lodge, Bridge-water Road, Weybridge, Surrey KT13 0ED.
The index is also available online (pay-for-view) at:
<www.familyhistoryonline.net/database/ WMiddlesexFHSmar.shtml>

Middlesex 1813-1837. For those parishes outside the City of London not in Boyd or Pallot (see page 20). 60% to date but many from BTs only, hence gaps. Year only for small parishes, year and month for large (in advanced preparation for publication on CD).
West Surrey FHS, c/o 17 Lane End Drive, Knaphill, Woking, Surrey GU21 2QQ

Chiswick Marriages *(West Middx FHS).* Around 800 marriages October 1678 - December 1800. Enquiries giving approx date £1.00 plus SAE or 5 $US/Can. No SAE required.
A.E. Powell, 71 Whitestile Road, Brentford, Middlesex TW8 9NR.

St Paul, Hammersmith Feb 1664/5-June 1837 (Card Index).
Hammersmith and Fulham Archives and Local History Centre, The Lilla Huset, 191 Talgarth Rd., London W6 8BJ.
email: *archives@lbhf.gov.uk*

Harlington Parish Registers. *(West Middx FHS)* Baptisms, marriages and burials **1540-1850**. Enquiries: £1.00.
Mr P. Sherwood, 5 Victoria Lane, Harlington, Middlesex UB3 5EW.

Hayes, St Mary's Parish Registers *(West Middx FHS).*
Baptisms, Marriages and Burials; **1557-1840**. Enquiries: £1.00 per surname.
Hillingdon Parish Registers. *(West Middx FHS).* Baptisms **1559-1909**; Marriages **1559-1910**; Burials **1559-1948** (churchyard) and **1867-1903** (cemetery). Enquiries: £1.00.
Isleworth All Saints Parish Registers. Baptisms **1566-1852**; Marriages **1566-1895**; Burials **1566-1879**. Enquiries: £1.00.
Mrs M Sibley, 13 Blossom Way, West Drayton, Middlesex UB7 9HF.

Isleworth Parish Church. Marriages 1754-1895.
Further details from:
Mr A.E. Powell, as above.

MANCHESTER, GREATER, and MERSEYSIDE
See under **Lancashire**

MIDDLESEX
See under **London and Middlesex**

MIDLANDS, WEST
See under **Warwickshire, Staffordshire** and **Worcestershire**

MONMOUTHSHIRE (Gwent)
See under **Wales**

NORFOLK

Published Registers. Many published registers and indexes are listed in S.A. Raymond, *Norfolk: a genealogical bibliography.* FFHS, 1993.

The Parish Register Transcription Society has transcribed many Norfolk parish registers, which are now available on CD.
Website: **<www.prtsoc.org.uk/>**

Norfolk Marriage Index 1801-18
Norfolk Record Office, Gildengate House, Anglia Square, Upper Green Lane, Norwich NR3 1AX
webpage:
<www.archives.norfolk.gov.uk/nroindex.htm>
email: *norfrec@norfolk.gov.uk*

Norfolk Marriage Index 1801-1837. CD. *(Norfolk FHS.).*
Webpage: **<www.norfolkfhs.org.uk/sales/ marriageindex.htm>**

Phillimore's marriage registers. List of registers available.
<www.origins.org.uk/genuki/NFK/norfolk/ church/phillimore.shtml>

Boyd. In Main Series. 275 parishes, approx. 38% of county (many less than full coverage). Note. There are two sets of volumes.
Boyd's Marriage index Norfolk 1751-1837.
Great Yarmouth Central Library, Tolhouse Street, Great Yarmouth, Norfolk NR30 2SH

Pallot. 132 parishes.

NORTHAMPTONSHIRE

Northamptonshire Marriage Index.
1707-1812. Almost complete, with many marriages much earlier, a few parishes back to the beginning.
1813-1837. Complete. This index, complied by Mr C. Bollen Blore, is now operated by *Northamptonshire Record Office.* Postal enquiries only. No charge for short searches. Fee from £5.00 for longer searches (over half an hour). SAE required, no smaller than A5.
Northamptonshire Record Office, Wootton Hall Park, Northampton NN4 8BQ.
email: *archivist@northamptonshire.gov.uk*
Webpage: **<www.northamptonshire.gov.uk/ Community/record/about_us.htm>**

Northamptonshire continued

Marriage Index. *(Northamptonshire FHS).* Ongoing project to index registers, 1756-1837. Search service available for completed parishes.
Mr P. Wilkins, 19 Pound Lane, Bugbrooke, Northants NN7 3RH.
Webpage: **<www.northants-fhs.org>** (click on 'Search services')

Marriage Licence Card Index 1598-1685. Held at Northamptonshire CRO. This is being indexed by groom or bride and by date.
email: *audreybuxton@supanet.com*

Boyd. In Miscellaneous Series. 43 parishes, approx. 14% of the county.

Pallot. 37 parishes.

NORTHUMBERLAND
(Newcastle and Tyneside now in Tyne and Wear)

Newcastle Register Office Indexes. An online index to registers of births and marriages held by district registrars, from 1837. Incomplete as yet.
Webpages: **<www.ndfhs.org.uk/RegIndex.html>**
<www.newcastle.gov.uk/core.nsf/a/ dfcdeathshistorical>

Northumberland and Durham Marriages *(Northumberland and Durham FHS).* This database contains 264,274 marriage entries from the registers of 124 parishes from the County Durham and 103 parishes from Northumberland. Pay-per-view.
Webpage: **<www.familyhistoryonline.net/ database/NDFHSmar.shtml>**

Meldon, 1706-1812. *Morpeth Herald* **April 1860- March 1865.** Births, Deaths and Marriages, available for searches.
Felton and Swarland Local History Society, Peter Cook, Project Leader, 23 Benlaw Grove, Felton, Morpeth, Northumberland NE65 9NG.
Webpage: **<www.genuki.bpears.org.uk/NBL/ FeltonLHS.html>**

Published registers *(Northumberland and Durham FHS).* Many indexed transcripts covering the whole of the county, published on m'fche.
N. & D. FHS, 2nd Floor, Bolbec Hall, Westgate Rd, Newcastle upon Tyne NE1 1SE.
Webpage:
<www.ndfhs.org.uk/Sales/prices/NI_03.html>

Co. Durham Index. Earliest date to 1837. Index now includes 16 Northumberland parishes along the north bank of the Tyne from the Cumberland border (19,800). Details as under Co. Durham.
Compiled by the late W.E. Rounce, now held by N&D FHS, as above.

Northumberland continued

Original Indexes: publications on m'fiche:
Pre-1837 Non-Anglican Marriages; Northumberland Marriages 1798-1812 (not in Boyd's Index); The Deaneries of Alnwick 1813-1839; Bamburgh 1813-1839; Bedlington; Bellingham; Corbridge; Hexham; Morpeth, Newcastle Central; Newcastle West; Norham; Tynemouth; all for the years 1813-1839. Publications (on CD) Northumberland Marriages 1813-1837 indexed by George Bell, Berwick on Tweed Marriages 1572-1700 (DNPRS), Newcastle St Nicholas Marriages 1574-1812 (DNPRS). These are now available from *Ancestral Indexes eShop*.
Webpage: <**www.ancestral-indexes.co.uk**>

Boyd. In Main Series. 84 parishes, approx. 73% of the county.

Joiner. 100 parishes; 82918 entries.

Pallot. 15 parishes.

NOTTINGHAMSHIRE

Nottinghamshire FHS Marriage Index.
Marriages for the whole county from the beginning of parish registers to 1837 have been indexed as follows:
1813-1837. Whole county indexed and available on m'fche only. From beginning of registers up to 1812 Phillimore series covers a lot of the county. M'fche of the Phillimore vols. and indexes to them are available. Parishes not included in Phillimore have been indexed and are available in three periods - up to 1699; 1700-1753 and 1754-1812. A new series, starting with marriages of 19th century Nottingham churches, is now available on m'fche from the start of the register up to 1900. This includes the registers of two Catholic parishes - Nottingham and Mansfield.

Notts Victorian Marriages. *(publications on m'fche from Notts FHS)*.
Fiche 1. Aslockton 1894, Brinsley 1861, Bulcote 1841, Carlton St Paul 1883, Cinderhill Christchurch 1896, Daybrook St Paul 1896, Harby 1867, Hucknall Torkard St John 1884.
Fiche 2. Carrington St John 1847, Kimberley 1848.
Fiche 3. Mapperley St June 1881, Netherfield 1886, Pleasley Hill 1897, Retford St Saviour 1868, Scofton with Osberton 1878.

Nottinghamshire Marriages CD. Over 345,000 entries.
Mrs S. Greenall, 10 Sherwin Walk, St. Anns, Nottingham NG3 1AH.
email: shopmanager@nottsfhs.org.uk
Webpage: <**www.nottsfhs.org.uk**>
(click on 'Shop' or 'Research')

Nottinghamshire continued

Nottingham, 1562-1812. Ts and Ms indexes to *Phillimore Parish Register series* for Nottingham St. Mary 1566-1813; St. Peter 1572-1812; St. Nicholas 1562-1812. Askham *c.*1754-1902, Barton in Fabis 1558-1997, Carburton 1528-1812, Clarborough c1754-c1901, Costock 1558-1990, Cossal 1755-1837, Eakring 1563-1700, East Leeke 1600-1900, East Retford *c.*1754-1900, Edingley 1580-1837, Edwinstowe 1634-1758, Flintham 1600-1899, Gedling 1556-1841, Gotham 1558-1999, Kingston-on-Soar 1630-1996, Kirklington 1575-1837, Linby 1692-1812, Mansfield St Peter 1777-1780, Mansfield Woodhouse *c.*1863-1897, Newark 1798-1839, Nottingham Holy Trinity 1842-1956, Papplewick 1661-1812, Rempstone 1570-1990, South Muskham 1659-1812, Stanford on Soar 1633-1992, Strelly 1665-1812, Walesby 1580-1792, Walkeringham 1613-1870, Wellow 1703-1812, West Leake 1616-1835, Winkburn 1740-1837, Worksop 1558-1838.
Nottinghamshire Archives, County House, Castle Meadow Road, Nottingham NG2 1AG.
webpage:
<**www.nottinghamshire.gov.uk/libraries/ Archives**>
email: *archives@nottscc.gov.uk*

Boyd. In Miscellaneous Series, 161 parishes, approx. 68% of the county. Mainly 1651-1675, 1701-1725.

Joiner. 164 parishes; 125223 entries.

Pallot. Most of county.

OXFORDSHIRE

Published Registers. Many published registers are listed in S.A. Raymond, *Oxfordshire: a genealogical bibliography*. FFHS, 1994.

Oxfordshire FHS Index. Complete for whole (pre-1974) county for both parties, **1538-1837** (*c.*320,000 entries). Computer searches £1.50 + SAE for a specified marriage or £1.50 + SAE per surname for up to 60 references for either male or female marriages. The period covered can be specified to reduce numbers listed. Also on m'fche and CD.
M'fche copies for public use are at *Oxfordshire Record Office, St Luke's Church, Temple Road, Cowley, Oxford OX4 2HT*, and the *Centre for Oxfordshire Studies Library, Westgate, Oxford OX1 1DJ* (long-term 'refurbishment' closure imminent).
Dr. Alan Simpson, Forest Farmhouse, Old Road, Shotover Hill, Headington, Oxford OX3 8TA.
Webpage:
<**searches.oxfordshirefhs.org.uk/#marrs**>

Mormon Index. 1538-1837, both parties. Mainly north of county. 142 parishes (57% of county) but many part-period only, listed in *Guide to Boyd* and in *Oxon PRs and BTs* (also in *The Phillimore Atlas and Index of Parish Registers*, as if part of Boyd). From orig. regs., BTs and printed sources. Year only. Phonetic. Superseded by Oxon FHS Index, but available in TS at *Oxfordshire Record Office*, entries also included in IGI.
Oxfordshire Record Office (as above).
Webpage: <**www.oxfordshire.gov.uk/oro**>
email: *Archives@Oxfordshire.gov.uk*

Boyd. See Mormon Index, above.

Pallot. 16 parishes.

RUTLAND
(see also Leicestershire, pages 19-20)

Rutland Marriage Index 1538-1754. For details of the progress of this index and purchase on CD contact:
email: *audreybuxton@supanet.com*

Rutland Marriage Index 1754-1837 *(Leicestershire and Rutland FHS)*. Publications on m'fche:
Volume 1: Empingham, Essendine, Great Casterton, Ketton, Normanton, Pickworth, Rhyall, Tickencote Tinwell, Tixover;
Volume 2: Barrowden, Edith Weston, Glaston, Hambleton, Lyndon, Manton, North Luffenham, Pilton, South Luffenham, Wing;
Volume 3: Ayston, Bisbrooke, Caldecott, Lyddington, Seaton, Stoke Dry,Uppingham;
Volume 4: Belton, Braunston, Egleton, Oakham, Preston, Ridlington, Wardley;
Volume 5: Burley, Clipsham, Exton, Greetham, Stretton, Thistleton, Whitwell, (No registers for Horn);
Volume 6: Ashwell, Cottesmore, Langham, Market Overton, Teigh, Whissendine;
Leicester and Rutland FHS, Research Centre. Freeschool Lane, Leicester.
email: *secretary@lrfhs.org.uk*
Webpage: <**www.lrfhs.net/onlinesales.htm**>
(click on 'Microfiche online sales').

CD publications from Leicester and Rutland FHS.
Leicestershire and Rutland "strays" marriages. Over 13,000 marriages.
Rutland parish registers. 55,000 entries from 20 parishes.
Webpage: <**www.lrfhs.net/onlinesales.htm**>
(click on 'CD ROM publications').

Boyd. In Miscellaneous Series. 23 parishes, approx. 38% of the county.

SHROPSHIRE
The **Shropshire Parish Register Society** published many transcripts and indexes of parish registers, which are sometimes available in reference libraries.

Shropshire Marriage Indexes. Many offline indexes are listed at:
<**www.genuki.org.uk:8080/big/eng/SAL/ MarriageIndexes.html**>

Gwynne Index Shropshire, 1813-1837. Complete. Both parties. Orig. regs. 70%, microfilm 10% printed sources 10%, other transcripts 10%. Complete date. Widows shown. Alphabetical. 36,500 marriages in 220 parishes. It includes marriages from a number of border parishes but no strays. Further details from:
R.W. Gwynne, 26 Derwent Close, Dane Bank, Denton, Manchester M34 2FW.

The Lewis Index Shropshire 1750-1812. This index was compiled by Mr M.G. Lewis for all those parishes not covered by Boyd's Marriage Index. It includes full details of the marriage as outlined in the Parish Registers. In addition the index incorporates over 5,000 'strays' for any date up to 1837 i.e. Salopians who married outside Shropshire. Widows where identified as such in the PR's and brides who married away from their own parish are also indexed, but brides who married in their own parish are not indexed separately. There are also a few entries prior to 1750 but these are mostly for N.E. Shropshire. Multiple entries by negotiation. Cheques made payable to Mrs. M. Lewis.
The Lewis Marriage Index, The Berringtons, Woodseaves, Market Drayton, Shropshire TF9 2AU.

North Wales Marriage Index. The Marches. 20 ancient and 2 modern parishes on and around the Welsh border, 70% from transcripts supplemented by St. Asaph diocese marriage bonds. Other details as Flintshire. Details of parishes covered and costs from:
Mr Dafydd Hayes, Pen Y Cae, Ffordd Hendy, Gwernymynydd, Sir y Fflint CH7 5JP.

Boyd. In Main Series. 126 parishes, approx. 49% of county. Incl. all those registers which had been printed by the Shropshire P.R. Society before 1929. Copies at *Shropshire Archives, Shrewsbury* and *Guildhall Library, London*; in addition to *Society of Genealogists*.

Pallot. 115 parishes.

SOMERSET

Published Registers. Many published registers are listed in: S.A. Raymond, *Somerset: a genealogical bibliography.* FFHS, 1991.

Bath BMD: Births, Marriages and Deaths on the Internet. Online index to civil registers held by district registrars.
Webpage: <**www.bathbmd.org.uk**>

Somerset Marriage Index, 1754-1837 *(Somerset and Dorset FHS).* Card slip index covering the whole of the old county. Both parties. Alphabetical. Single entry search, £1.00 for members £2.00 non-members + SAE or 2 IRCs. One surname searches not available to non-members. A list of parishes included in the Marriage Index is also available, at a cost of £2.00 + 33p postage. Please make cheques, money orders etc, to
S&D FHS Somerset Marriage Co-ordinator, Bernard Welchman, The Cottage, Manor Terrace, Paignton, Devon, TQ3 3RQ.
Webpage: <**www.sdfhs.org/Sommarr.htm**>
email: *B@bdwfh.com*
This index is also available online, pay-per-view.
Website: <**www.familyhistoryonline.net/database/SomersetDorsetFHSmarpost.shtml**>

Somerset Marriage Index pre-1754 *(Somerset and Dorset FHS).* Young rapidly growing index. Covers the whole of the old county. Single entry search £1.50. One name searches not available to non-members.
Judy Hodges, Flat 21, Thornton Lodge, 24-26 Thornton Hill, London SW19 4HS.
Webpage: <**www.sdfhs.org/pre1754.htm**>
email: *judy@lodge2199.freeserve.co.uk*
This index is also available online, pay-per-view.
Website: <**www.familyhistoryonline.net/database/SomersetDorsetFHSmarpre.shtml**>

Somerset Marriage Indexes *(Somerset and Dorset FHS).* Taunton St. Mary 1558-1754 (3 vols); Taunton St. James 1610-1754 (3 vols) book and m'fche.
Mrs M. Monk, 65 Wyke Rd., Weymouth DT4 9QN.
email: *a.monk@btinternet.com*
Webpage: <**www.sdfhs.org/Pubs.htm**>

North Somerset Marriage Index. Index by male surname to registers for Somerset parishes formerly in Avon, **1754-1837.** A comparable index for the rest of the county, by male and female surnames, is held by the Somerset and Dorset FHS.
Somerset Record Office, Obridge Road, Taunton TA2 7PU.
webpage: <**www.somerset.gov.uk/archives**>
(click 'search catalogues and indexes').
email: *Archives@somerset.gov.uk*

Dr. Campbell's Index. Index, by surname of baptisms and marriages in the parishes of South and West Somerset, as far east as Martock, Ilminster, Langport etc., from beginning of registers to 1899. Excludes Minehead, Taunton, Wilton, Wellington and Bridgewater, and marriages covered by Phillimore's *'Somerset Marriages'* (15 vols. **1898-1915**).
Somerset Record Office, as left.

Bath and Wells Diocese Marriage Index. Covers diocese, almost co-terminous with County of Somerset. Males only. **1813-1837**, 99.9% coverage; **1754-1812** 95% coverage. Approx. 65% of earlier registers covered (where surviving and BTs if not). Mainly from original regs. All information except witnesses shown. Alphabetical. List available. SAE please for request or quote.
G.S.W. Smith, Middle Whites Farm, Burtle, Bridgwater, Som. TA7 8NH.

The Marriage Index for Bristol and Avon, 1754-1837 *(Bristol and Avon FHS).* Covers all parishes in Bristol and Avon for **1754 - 1837**, with some earlier material for certain parishes and Quaker marriages. Currently being re-checked against the original registers so that it can be published on CD.
The first CD, covering the Bristol Diocese from 1813 to 1837, has now been published. Details can be found on the website. Checks can be still be made against the original index. The normal charge is £2 for each individual marriage enquiry.
Mrs Janet Hiscocks, "Beanacre", Easter Compton, Bristol, BS35 5RJ
email: *toresearch@bafhs.org.uk*
Website:
<**www.bafhs.org.uk/shop/marriages.htm**>

Somerset Genweb Marriage Index: Bristol and Somerset. Online index of submitted entries.
<**www.rootsweb.com/%7Eengsom/marriages**>

Boyd. In Main Series. 123 parishes, approx. 24% of the county.

Pallot. 152 parishes.

SOUTH YORKSHIRE
See **Yorkshire, West Riding**

STAFFORDSHIRE

(Walsall and Wolverhampton area now in West Midlands)

Staffordshire BMD: Births, Marriages and Deaths on the Internet. Index to civil registers held by district registrars, 1837-1950+. Includes over 450,000 marriages.
<web1.netnation.com/~bmsgh/staffsbmd/>

West Midlands BMD: Births, Marriages and Deaths on the Internet. Index to civil registers held by district registrars, covering the southern part of Staffordshire as well as parts of Warwickshire and Worcestershire. Includes over 400,000 marriages. Webpage: <www.bmsgh.org/wmbmd>

Published Registers. Many registers have been published by the Staffordshire Parish Register Society.
Webpage:

Staffordshire Marriage Index (B&MSGH). Ancient county, plus detached area in Worcs. County coverage complete. Both parties to June 1837. From transcripts, registers, BTs. All details as given in entry, i.e. status, occupation, consent of, lic., but no clergy or witnesses. Alphabetical. Similar names searched. List of parishes on request with SAE. £3.00 per specific item, one-name lists £3 per 50 items and pro rata basic statement. Full details of entry given from IGI entry. SAE with all enquiries or 3 IRCs. Cheques made out to BandMSGH please.
Mrs C. Smith, 5 Woodhayes Road, Wednesfield, Wolverhampton, West Midlands WV11 1AD.
Webpage:
<www.bmsgh.org/search/st_marr_Index.html>
This index is also available online, pay-per-view. Webpage: <www.familyhistoryonline.net/ database/BMSGHSTSMar.shtml>

Greater Birmingham Marriage Index, 1776-1837. (B&MSGH). Includes the Staffordshire parishes of Harborne and Handsworth. See under Warwickshire for details.

Boyd. Miscellaneous Series, 4 parishes.

Pallot. 24 parishes.

SUFFOLK

Information. For more detailed information on indexes both published and unpublished see the leaflet *Indexes for the Suffolk Family Historian*, 2nd edition Nov. 1998, compiled by Susan Bourne. £1.50 incl. post.
26 Brookside Road, Istead Rise, Northfleet, Kent DA13 9JJ.

Published Registers. Many published parish registers for Suffolk are listed in S.A. Raymond, *Suffolk: a genealogical bibliography.* FFHS., 1992.

Suffolk continued

Suffolk Marriage Index (Suffolk FHS). This index has 25,317 entries from 1536-1902, and cover 32 parishes. In progress. Pay-per-view.
Webpage: <www.familyhistoryonline.net/ database/SFKMarriageIndex.shtml>

Suffolk Marriage Index 1813-1837 (Suffolk FHS). 99% coverage of the County. £1 per search for up to 5 entries, state names, geographical area and date. Please include SAE or 2 IRC's. Published, below. Available on Family History Online, pay-per-view.
Webpage: <www.familyhistoryonline.co.uk/ database/SFKMarr1813.shtml>

Compilation of **1754-1812** in progress, as yet unchecked but a look-up service is available. Also **pre 1753** in progress but not complete. £1 per search for up to 5 entries, state names, geographical area and date. Please include SAE or 2 IRCs.
Mrs Pamela Palgrave, Crossfield House, Dale Rd, Stanton, Bury St. Edmunds, Suffolk IP31 2DY.
Webpage: <www.suffolkfhs.co.uk/service.html>

Suffolk FHS publications. The **1813-37** index (above) is published (book and m'fche) in 17 volumes arragned by Deanery. A variety of parish registers are available on CD.
Webpage: <www.suffolkfhs.org.uk/public.html>

Suffolk Marriage Transcripts. Available to purchase on CD.
Lakenheath Parish Registers **Marriages 1712-1922.** Bishops Transcripts **1638-1720.**
Hundon Parish Registers **1676-1836, 1837-1910, Banns 1837-1861, 1862-1913.**
Hundon Independent Chapel **Marriages 1883-1904.**
Stradishall Parish Church **Marriages 1600-1836**
For further details of these and other records available on these CDs contact:
Mr Norman Hunt, 22 Tiberius Close, Haverhill, Suffolk CB9 0NP.

Colneis Peninsular Marriages 1700-1837 and births and burials. (Felixstowe FHS). Searches possible for a fee of £1.50 payable to the society.
Mrs J.S. Campbell, 7 Victoria Road, Felixstowe, Suffolk IP11 7PT.

The Cosford Database. Includes marriages for parishes in the Cosford district.
Webpage: <www.cosford-database.co.uk>

A Selection of Military Marriages. Indexed from Newspapers and Books. Mainly covering Suffolk with a few other counties and countries.
Webpage:
<homepages.rootsweb.com/~mwi/milmarr.txt>

Boyd. In Main Series. 489 parishes and one Society of Friends' meeting. Approx. 98% of county, but many pre-1754 only. Copies of this Index are available in the three branches of *Suffolk Record Office.*

Pallot. 49 parishes.

SURREY

Published Registers. Many published registers are listed in S.A. Raymond, *Surrey and Sussex parish registers, monumental inscriptions and wills.* FFHS, 2001.

Surrey Marriage Index to 1937. CD. More than 162,100 marriages in mainly rural Surrey. However, included are: over 1,100 marriages in Battersea (1802-1837); over 10,000 in Bermondsey (1609-74 and 1740-1832); over 5,500 in Camberwell (1601-1812); over 1,500 in Lambeth (1716-24, 1826, 1830-1831); over 500 in Southwark, Christ Church (1807-1812) and over 3000 in Southwark St Saviour (1605-1625). There are no marriages for Newington, Rotherhithe, Streatham or Wandsworth.
West Surrey FHS, c/o 17 Lane End Drive, Knaphill, Woking, Surrey GU21 2QQ
Webpage: <www.wsfhs.org/IndexesResearch.htm>

Selon Index. Ten parishes, original registers, including St. Mark Kennington (BTs recently discovered), all within metropolitan area. Mostly to 1837. Minimum fee, £5 + SAE.
Peter R. Shilham, 6 Beckford Close, Wokingham, Berks. RG41 1HN.

Thames Riverside Parish Series - see under Kent, page 16.

Name Index for Kingston Churches. Marriages and Baptisms and Burials. 1850-1900. Kingston University Database.
Kingston Museum and Heritage Service, Local History Room, North Kingston Centre, Richmond Rd., Kingston KT2 5PE.
Webpage: <localhistory.kingston.ac.uk/contributePages/datasets.html>

Original Parish Register Facsimiles *(NW Kent FHS).* These CDs are facsimiles of the actual parish registers and are not name-indexed.
Darenth: St Margaret Marriages **1813-1954** and Burials **1813-1992.**
Dartford: Holy Trinity Marriages **1813-1984.**
Horton Kirby: St Mary Marriages **1813-1954** and Burials **1813-2000.** Further details and prices from:
Mrs Barbara Attwaters, 141 Princes Road, Dartford, Kent DA1 3HJ.
Webpage: <www.nwkfhs.org.uk/pub_pr.htm>

Canterbury Peculiars Marriage Licence Index.
A surname index to the marriage licences issued in various peculiars which came under the jurisdiction of the Archbishop of Canterbury. These peculiars included the Deanery of Croydon (Surrey and Middlesex). *Lambeth Palace Library* have completed the index for Bocking (Essex)..

Boyd. In Miscellaneous Series. 69 parishes, approx. 45% of the county.

Pallot. 36 parishes.

SUSSEX

Published Registers. Many published registers are listed in S.A. Raymond, *Surrey and Sussex parish registers, monumental inscriptions and wills.* FFHS, 2001.

The Parish Register Transcription Society has transcribed many West Sussex parish registers, which are now available on CD.
Website:

Sussex Marriage Index 1538-1837. Both parties; 100% coverage. Incl. Fleet Prison. Sussex parties married in London, Middx., Surrey or Kent. Also includes marriage allegations and Roman Catholic and Quaker marriages. Complete date. Widows shown. Phonetic arrangement. Available on CD with parish coverage in detail and with distribution maps details from:- *SFHG, 40 Tanbridge Park, Horsham, West Sussex RH12 1SZ.*
Webpage:
<www.sfhg.org.uk/marriageindex.html>

Allegations for Marriage Licences Issued by the Commissary Court of Surrey between 1673-1770. Searchable online database.
Webpage: <www.newenglandancestors.org/research/database/vr_surreymarriages/default.asp>

Marriage Licences. Chichester archdeaconry, published to 1800; index 1801-40 (6,000) cards. Deaneries of Chichester and Pagham and Tarring, pub to 1730; index 1731-1840 (6,000) cards.
West Sussex R.O., County Hall, Chichester, West Sussex PO19 1RN.
Webpage:<www.westsussex.gov.uk/ccm/content/libraries-and-archives/record-office/family-history/marriage-licences.en>
email: *recordsoffice@westsussex.gov.uk*

Billingshurst, Sussex, Marriage. Indexes 4,958 marriages, 1575 to 1899. Pay per view.
Website: <www.familyhistoryonline.net/database/SSXBillingshurstMar.shtml>

East Hoathley Registers, Baptisms, Banns, Marriages and Burials.
A charge of £5.00 per surname printout. Searches for single individuals free.
Jane Seabrook, The White House, 20 High Street, East Hoathley, Nr. Lewes, East Sussex BN8 6EB.
email: *claras@netway.co.uk*

Boyd. In Miscellaneous Series. 57 parishes, approx. 17% of the county.

Pallot. 27 parishes.

WARWICKSHIRE

(Birmingham and Coventry area now in West Midlands)

West Midlands BMD: Births, Marriages and Deaths on the Internet.
Index to civil registers held by district registrars, including RDs in the Birmingham area (which also includes parts of Staffordshire and Worcestershire). Webpage: <**www.bmsgh.org/wmbmd/**>

Warwickshire Marriage Index (B&MSGH). Covers county, excluding those parishes in Greater Birmingham Index. Both parties. 1800-1837 (99% coverage); 1754-1799 (96%); pre-1754 (24%). Mainly from orig. regs., some printed sources and BTs. Complete date. Widows shown. Alphabetical. List available. Fees (payable to B&MSGH) as for Greater Birmingham Index (see below).
Mrs Gwen Wilkins, 1 Hurley Close, Leamington Spa CV32 5XB.
Webpage:
<**www.bmsgh.org/search/Wa_marr_index.html**>

Warwickshire Parish Registers (B&MSGH). Only Hockley St George, 1830-37 at present, but more promised. Pay-per-view.
Webpage: <**www.familyhistoryonline.net/ database/BMSGHWARpr.shtml**>

Rugby District Parish Registers (Rugby Family History Group). Currently only the parish of Dunchurch St Peter, 1538-1837, is included in this database. Pay-per-view.
Website: <**www.familyhistoryonline.net/ database/RugbyFHGprs.shtml**>

Warwick St. Mary Marriage Index. 1651-1711.
Warwickshire County Record Office.

Warwickshire: St. Matthew, Walsall, Marriages 1663-1754 and 1754-1837 comp. Malcolm Cooper.
Walsall Local History Centre, Essex Street, Walsall WS2 7AS.

Greater Birmingham Marriage Index, 1801-1837 (B&MSGH). Both parties. Covers the Birmingham parishes of St. Martin, St. Philip, St. George, St. Thomas, and All Saints, together with Warw. parishes of Aston, Edgbaston and Sheldon; Worcs. parishes of Kings Norton, Northfield, and Yardley; and Staffs. parishes of Handsworth and Harborne, together with Quaker and RC regs. Mostly orig. regs. Complete. Widows shown. Charges £3.00 search fee for each surname which includes up to 3 entries from the index. Additional entries 20p each. BandMSGH members receive 20% discount when quoting membership number. Cheques to B&MSGH and enclose SAE or 2 IRC's.
Mrs P. Archer, 56 St. Andrew's Road, Lillington, Leamington Spa CV32 7EX.
Also available pay-per-view on the Family History Online webpage:
<**www.familyhistoryonline.co.uk/database/ BMSGHBirmMar.shtml**>

Index to Births, Marriages and Deaths. From the Warwick Advertiser. Includes 16,200 marriages (filed under both parties). Covers a wide area not only in Midlands but from wider afield. Probably many copied from other papers. SAE + £1 per name (in case of common names, christian name too)
Mrs P. Page, 218 Wake Green Road, Moseley, Birmingham B13 9QE.

Birth Marriage and Death Certificates. (BMSGH). Online pay per view index, consisting of 101,581 names taken from Birth, Marriage and Death Certificates and similar records donated to the Birmingham and Midland Society of Genealogy and Heraldry as being unrelated to the donor's research.
Webpage: <**www.familyhistoryonline.net/ database/UnrelatedCerts.shtml**>

Boyd. In Miscellaneous series. 30 parishes; approx 11% of county, many 1651-1675 only.

Pallot. 29 parishes.

WESTMORLAND

(now part of Cumbria)

Published Registers. Many published parish registers are listed in S.A. Raymond, Cumberland and Westmorland: a genealogical bibliography. FFHS, 1993.

Westmorland and North Lancashire Index, 1700-1837. Covers whole of Westmorland and the Furness and Cartmel area of Lancashire (now in Cumbria). Males only indexed. c.40,000 marriages. **1813-1837.** Complete coverage, earlier period c.80% coverage. Complete date, widows shown, and whether by lic. Arranged phonetically. Fee £5 minimum per search. List of entries for the same surname, an additional 50p per entry. Parish list sent with each enquiry.
S.G. Smith, 59 Friar Road, Orpington, Kent BR5 2BW.
email: *Sydney.smith7@ntlworld.com*

Boyd. In Miscellaneous Series. 13 parishes; approx. 16% of the county, pre-1719 only.

Joiner. 50 Parishes; 23,464 entries.

Pallot. 14 parishes.

WILTSHIRE

The Nimrod Index. A complete county Index of all marriages 1538-1837 (males and females). Taken from original registers, BTs and printed sources. Approx. 255,000 marriage, including approx. 5,200 strays. Search fees: £3.00 for individual person search. Complete surname listings generally £8:00 for single sex, £15:00 for both sexes, but contact for full details of prices.
David and Jenny Carter, Docton Court, 2 Myrtle Street, Appledore, Bideford, Devon EX39 1PH, UK.
webpage: <**www.NimrodResearch.co.uk**>
email: *enquiries@nimrodresearch.co.uk*

Marriage Licence Bonds for Sarum Diocese

1609-1837. (incl. Wiltshire, Berkshire and Dorset). *(Wiltshire FHS)*. CD; also available online. Over 70,000 bonds. Covers Wiltshire, most of Berkshire, part of Dorset, and Uffculme, Devon. Normally includes bridegroom's name, age, occupation, place of residence, marital state, Bride's name, age, place of residence and marital state: name of bondsmen, with occupations and place of residence. Possibly parish church(es) where the marriage could take place. In some cases the bond is the only record of the marriage. Available from:
Wiltshire FHS, 10 Castle Lane, Devizes, Wiltshire, SN10 1HJ.
Webpage for CD:
<www.wiltshirefhs.co.uk/mlb%20cd.htm>
Online Webpage:
<www.familyhistoryonline.net/database/ WIL_MLB.shtml>

Wiltshire Marriage Index. CD. Photocopies of Phillimores transcripts for Wiltshire also available.
Webpage: **<www.parishchest.com/en-gb/ dept_219.html>**

Boyd. In Miscellaneous Series. 73 parishes, approx. 21% of the county, but nearly all 1651-1675 only.

Pallot. 85 parishes.

WORCESTERSHIRE

Worcestershire Marriage Index 1660-1837

(B&MSGH). male and female searches done. Complete as far as is possible from Parish Registers, BTs, Bonds and Allegations and printed sources for all historic County parishes, including those lost or gained to Worcestershire. Includes Quaker and Roman Catholic marriages. Many strays included. Charges £3.00 per surname to include 3 entries. Next 47 entries 20p each. Thereafter ask for a quotation. Cheques payable to *BandMSGH*. Enclose SAE. Members are entitled to 20% dicount if they quote their membership number.
Mrs Angela Purcell, 8 Ironside Close, Bewdley, Worcs. DY12 2HX.
Webpage:
<www.bmsgh.org/search/Wo_marr_index.html>

Worcestershire Marriage Index.

The index contains all marriages from all churches in Worcestershire, including those lost or gained during boundary changes etc. plus Catholic and Quaker and other Non-Conformist churches. There is also an index for Brides **1701-1837** in book form.
Worcestershire Record Office H.Q., Worcester.

West Midlands BMD: Births, Marriages and Deaths on the Internet.

Index to civil registers held by district registrars, including RDs in North-East Worcestershire, as well as in parts of Staffordshire and Warwickshire.
Webpage: **<www.bmsgh.org/wmbmd/>**

Worcestershire Marriages. *(BandMSGH)*. This index consists of 163,168 records of marriage including at least one spouse from Worcestershire. Pay-per-view.
Webpage: **<www.familyhistoryonline.net/ atabase/BMSGHWORmar.shtml>**

Greater Birmingham Marriage Index, 1801-1837. 79,977 entries from the Greater Birmingham area, inc. Worcs. parishes of Kings Norton, Northfield, and Yardley. See under Warwickshire.
Webpage: **<www.familyhistoryonline.net/ database/BMSGHBirmMar.shtml>**

Boyd. In Miscellaneous Series. 47 parishes, but many **1651-1675** only.

Pallot. 37 parishes.

YORKSHIRE

Yorkshire BMD: Births Marriages and Deaths on the Internet.

Index to civil registers held by district registrars; 780,000+ marriages.
Webpage: **<www.yorkshirebmd.org.uk/>**

Barnsley Indexing Project *(Barnsley MBC/ Barnsley FHS)*. Online index to civil registers held by District Registrar. In progress.
Webpage:
<applications.barnsley.gov.uk/service/registrars/>

Rotherham MBC Searches and Index. Online index to civil registers held by district registrars. In progress.
Webpage: **<www.rotherham.gov.uk/graphics/ YourCouncil/Register+Office/Researching+Your +Family+Tree/>** (click 'searches and Index')

Sheffield City Council Index of Births Marriages and Deaths. Online index to civil registers held by district registrars. In progress.
Webpage: **<libplugins.sheffield.gov.uk/bmd/>**

The Tees Valley Indexes. Indexes to civil registers of the District Registrars of Middlesbrough, Hartlepool, Stockton on Tees, and Redcar and Cleveland. In progress.
Webpage: **<www.middlesbrough-indexes.co.uk/>**

Yorkshire continued

Published Registers, Indexes, etc. Numerous parish registers have been published by the Yorkshire Parish Register Society, its successor, the Parish Register Section of the Yorkshire Archaeological Society, and a variety of other publishers. These are fully listed in S.A. Raymond, *Yorkshire parish registers, monumental inscriptions and wills*. FHS., 2000.

Details of published registers currently available from the **Yorkshire Archaeological Society** are provided on their webpage:
<www.yorkshireparishregisters.com/index.htm>

Boyd. In Main Series. 44 parishes. Grooms only. A copy of this index is in York City Library.

Joiner. East Riding 223 parishes, 137,662 entries; 662 entries; North Riding 207 parishes; 108323 entries; West Riding 100 parishes, 171,342 entries.

Pallot. 21 parishes.

Archbishop of York's Marriage Bonds and Allegations. These are held by the *Borthwick Institute*, and were published in the *Yorkshire Archaeological journal*, vols.7-17, 1882-1908. A separate index was published as: *A consolidated index to Paver's marriage licences (1567 to 1630)* printed in the *Yorkshire Archaeological journal*. Yorkshire Archaeological Society, 1912. This is continued for 1630-1714 as Clay, John Wm. *Paver's marriage licences*. Yorkshire Archaeological Society record series vols.40, 43 and 46. 1909-12. The Borthwick Institute has published a further nine volumes taking the indexing from 1660 up to 1839: Newsome, E.B., et al. *An index to the Archbishop of York's marriage bonds and allegations* ... 1986-2003. The entries for 1567-1628 are online:
<www.genuki.org.uk/big/eng/YKS/Misc/Transcriptions/YKS/PaversIndex.html>
Borthwick Institute Website:
<www.york.ac.uk/inst/bihr/>

York City Marriage Index 1701-1837. Search service.
City of York and District Family History Society, The Research Room, The Raylor Centre, James Street, York YO10 3DW.
Webpage:
<www.yorkfamilyhistory.org.uk/searchservice.htm>
For m'fiche, contact:
Mrs Carol Mennell, 4 Orchard Close, Dringhouses, York YO24 2NX.
Webpage:
<www.yorkfamilyhistory.org.uk/publications.htm>

North Yorkshire and County Durham Marriages. *(Cleveland FHS).* Online pay per view index. For Northern Yorkshire the area of interest covers the region round Middlesbrough to Whitby on the east coast, across the North Yorks Moors to Thirsk then across county to the upper Dales in the west.
Webpage:<**www.familyhistoryonline.net/database/ClevelandFHSmar.shtml**>
Transcripts of registers are available on m'fiche; visit:
<**www.clevelandfhs.org.uk/Parish%20Register%20Transcripts.htm**>

Elland St Mary Marriage Registers (1649-1837). *(Calderdale FHS).* Online pay-per-view index. The Elland St. Mary's parish records for Marriages will contain over 15,410 records for people married between 1558 and 1837.
<**www.familyhistoryonline.net/database/CFHSEllandStMarysMarr.shtml**>

Halifax St. John's Marriage Registers. *(Calderdale FHS).* Online pay-per-view index. The Halifax St. John's parish records for marriages will contain nearly 32,000 records for people married between 1754 and 1837.
Webpage:<**www.familyhistoryonline.net/database/CFHSHalifaxStJohnsMarr.shtml**>
For 1813-1837, marriages are available on CD. Visit:<**www.cfhsweb.co.uk**>

Morley District Baptisms and Marriages. *(Morley FH Group).* Online pay per view index. The marriages cover Drighlington Nethertown URC 1869-1975, Gildersome St Peter's 1839-1914, Beeston Hill Methodist Chapel, Leeds, 1866-1898, Morley St. Paul's, 1878-1898, and Woodkirk St. Mary's, 1650-1837.
Webpage: <**www.familyhistoryonline.net/database/WRYMorley.shtml**>

Pontefract Marriages *(Pontefract FHS).* Online database; 15,980 marriage entries from 22 parishes in the Pontefract area, 1669 and 1918. Pay-per-view.
<**www.familyhistoryonline.net/database/PontefractDFHSmar.shtml**>

Wakefield District Marriages (1813-1837). *(Wakefield and District FHS).* Entries for *c.*20,202 marriages from 33 parishes in the Wakefield area, 1679 and 1992. Pay-per-view.
Webpage: <**www.familyhistoryonline.net/database/WakefieldDFHSmarB.shtml**>

Hereford Diocese, See under *Herefordshire*, page 25.

WALES

Note on placename spelling. In recent decades the accepted spelling of Welsh placenames has conformed (to an extent) to that approved by local Welsh authorities. However, in earlier centuries anglicised versions were used in the official records and catalogues likely to be used by historians.

In this Guide the latter are therefore generally used, except for 'Caernarvon(shire)', for which the Welsh spelling is 'Caernarfon(shire)' and the English was 'Carnarvonshire' (thus placing it alphabetically after 'Cardiganshire'). Nevertheless 'Caernarvonshire' is the spelling found in most atlases appearing up to 1974.

Church in Wales Records. Discussion of records at the National Library of Wales, with an index of pre-1838 marriage bonds.
<**www.llgc.org.uk/index.php?id=485andL**>

North Wales BMD: Births, Marriages and Deaths on the Internet. Index to the civil registers held by district registrars, from the family history societies of Clwyd, Gwynedd, and Montgomeryshire. Covers Anglesey, Caernarvonshire, Flintshire, Denbighshire, Merioneth and Montgomeryshire.
Webpage: <**www.northwalesbmd.org.uk**>

ANGLESEY

Gwynedd Marriage Index (Anglesey), 1754-1812, 1813-1837 *(Gwynedd FHS m'fche, see under Caernarvonshire).*

The North Wales Marriage Index, Part 4. 100% coverage of deposited PRs supplemented by BTs. Other details as Flintshire.
Dafydd Hayes, see Flintshire, page 32.

Anglesey County Record Office hold a list of 80 **parish registers** in their keeping for the Isle of Anglesey. These range in date from the earliest at Penrhosllugwy in 1578 up to 1997. Also **Bishop's transcripts** for Coedana, Ceirchiog, Heneglwys, Llanddeusant, Caergybi and Llanfachraeth.
County Record Office, Isle of Anglesy County Council, Council Offices, Llangefni LL77 7TW.
<**www.anglesey.gov.uk/doc.asp?cat=2583**>

BRECONSHIRE
(now part of Powys)

Breconshire Marriages pre-1754. Complete for all surviving Parish Registers and Bishop's Transcripts. Some checking still to be done. Further details from:
Diane Foster, Mansion View, Gwystre, Llandrindod Wells, Powys, Wales LD1 6RN.

Breconshire 1754-1812: Index complete by grooms only, Brides in process of being indexed. All information shown except names of witnesses. Searches free. £3.00 for providing details of successfully located marriage.
See webpage: <**mysite.wanadoo-members.co.uk/**

BreconSurnames>
which lists surnames to be found in this index. Please send SAE with postal enquiries.
Surnames A-L contact *A.A. Powell, MA, 24 Parc Bryn, Pontllanfraith, Blackwood, Gwent NP12 2RA.*
email: *alan@powellma.fsnet.co.uk*
Surnames **M-Z** contact *B. Hemmings, 1 Marianwen Street, Cefn Fforest, Blackwood, Gwent.*
email: *bryan@hemmings2002.freeserve.co.uk*

Breconshire continued

Breconshire 1813-1837. Index complete. Indexed by Groom and Bride. All information shown except names of witnesses. Searches free. £3.00 fee for providing details of successfully located marriage.
Contact details as for 1754-1812 Breconshire Marriage Index left

CAERNARVONSHIRE
(now part of Gwynedd)
See above for a note on alternative spellings.

Gwynedd Marriage Index (incl. Anglesey, Merioneth and part of Denbighshire) *(Gwynedd FHS m'fche publications)*
1. Llanbeblig (Caernarvon), 1754-1837.
2. County of **Anglesey**, all parishes 1813-1837.
3. Aberconwy (parishes in eastern Caernarvonshire and Denbighshire bordering on the Conwy River) 1813-1837.
4. Arfon (central Caernarvonshire all parishes) 1813-1837.
5. Dwyfor (western Caernarvonshire, all parishes) 1813-1837.
6. County of **Merioneth/Meirionnydd**, all parishes 1813-1837.
7. County of Anglesey, 1754-1812.
8. County of Merioneth/Meirionnydd 1754-1812 .
9. County of Anglesey 1813-1837.
Price list from:
Gwynedd F.H.S., 1 Tan-y-Cae, Bethel, Gwynedd, LL55 1YA, Wales.
Webpage: <**chtg.gwis.co.uk/**>
email: *gwyndaf@tan-y-cae.freeserve.co.uk.*

The North Wales Marriage Index, Part 4. 100% coverage of deposited PRs supplemented by BTs, and marriage bonds. Other details as Flintshire.
Dafydd Hayes, see Flintshire, page 32.

CARDIGANSHIRE

Three Counties Marriages 1813-1837 by Grooms Index. Covers Cardiganshire, Carmarthenshire and Pembrokeshire.
Webpage: <www.rootsweb.com/~wlscfhs/threecountiesmarriages1.htm>

Marriage Index (1813-1837). *(Dyfed FHS).* Online index to Cardiganshire grooms; includes indexes to marriages for each parish.
Webpage:
<www.dyfedfhs.org.uk/register/cgnmarri.htm>

Cardiganshire Marriages 1813-1837. *(Carmarthenshire FHS).* Online index.
Webpage:
<www.rootsweb.com/~wlscfhs/cdgmarr.pdf>

Cardiganshire Marriages 1813-1837 *(Dyfed FHS).*
Carmarthenshire Marriages 1813-1837
Pembrokeshire Marriages 1813-1837
Pembrokeshire Marriages pre 1813. All on CD.
Publications Officer:
Mrs E.A. Davies, Rhydybont, Bronwydd, Carmarthen, Carmarthenshire SA31 6HX.
Webpage: <www.dyfedfhs.org.uk/copi.htm>
See also
<www.genfair.com/shop/pages/cmn/page03.html>

Marriages Cardiganshire 1813-1875 *(Carmarthenshire FHS and Carmarthenshire Historical Society).*
Included in this index of South Wales are many baptisms, burials and other genealogical material.
Carmarthenshire FHS, PO Box 37, Aberystwyth SY23 2WL, Wales.
Webpage:
See also
(click on 'Family history societies')

Dyfed Marriages 1813-1837. *(Carmarthenshire FHS).* Published on CD. 45,000 marriages in one index, by groom, of Carmarthenshire, Cardiganshire and Pembrokeshire.
As above.

CARMARTHENSHIRE

Dyfed Marriage Index 1813-1837 *(Dyfed FHS).* (see entry under Cardiganshire).

The Merlin Indexes (publications on m'fche from *Dyfed FHS*) includes baptisms, marriages, burials, and vaccination records for parishes in Carmarthenshire (unless otherwise stated). The indexes also include some chapel registers, strays and banns.
Publications Officer: *Mrs E.A. Davies, Rhydybont, Bronwydd, Carmarthen, Carmarthenshire, SA33 6HX.*
Webpage: <www.dyfedfhs.org.uk/forsale4.htm>

Carmarthenshire 1754-1837, on m'fche.
West Glamorgan Archives Service, County Hall, Swansea.

See also under *Cardiganshire.*

DENBIGHSHIRE

The North Wales Marriage Index, Part 2. 100% coverage of deposited parish registers, supplemented by BTs, and marriage bonds. Other details as Flintshire.
Dafydd Hayes, see Flintshire, below.

Wrexham County Borough Council Marriage Index search facility. *(Clwyd FHS).* Index to marriage registers held by Wrexham Register Office.
Webpage: <www.wrexham.gov.uk/english/community/genealogy/MarriageIndexSearchForm.cfm>

Gwynedd Marriage Index. See under *Caernarvonshire.*

FLINTSHIRE

The North Wales Marriage Index, Part 1.
100% coverage of deposited parish registers, supplemented by BTs and marriage bonds. Year only, widows not shown. Post-1837 includes father's name. Alphabetical. Fees as per webpage.
Ann Hayes, Pen y Bryn, Mount Street, Ruthin, LL15 1BG.
Webpage:
<www.genfair.com/shop/pages/nwi/index.html>

GLAMORGAN

Glamorgan Marriage Index, pre 1837 *(Glamorgan FHS).* Whole county indexed males, females, parish. All 126 parishes. All extant PRs and BTs. Searches GFHS members only, no charge.
Mrs Kathleen Rhys, 12 The Green, Radyr, Cardiff CF15 8BR.
email: searches@glamfhs.info
Also available as an online pay per view database.
Webpage: <www.familyhistoryonline.co.uk/database/GLAMarriageIndex.shtml>

Marriage Index also available for purchase online or on m'fche. Full price list available. Updated CD version to be produced later.
Mrs Margaret Baird, 1 Dyfed House, Glenside Court, Ty Gwyn Road, Penylan, Cardiff CF23 5JS.
Webpage: <www.rootsweb.com/~wlsglfhs/>
The Parish Chest : <www.parishchest.com>
(click on 'Family History Societies')
Genfair webpage:
<www.genfair.com/shop/pages/gla/index.html>

Glamorgan continued

Glamorgan Area Marriages. Indexed from original parish records **1837-1900**. Commencing dates on marriages may vary for each parish. All parish marriages are on individual parish discs. **Marriages 1837-1900** from original registry office records. Merthyr Tydfil and Cardiff Nonconformist-Catholic- **Registry Office marriages 1837-1900**. All Nonconformist-Catholic-Registry Office Marriages are in a 10 Year Period On Disc.

For up-to-date listings and full details please send for leaflet or visit our webpage

Mrs Jennie Newman 9 Mylo Griffiths Close, Llandaff, Cardiff CF5 2RQ
email: *jennifer.newman@ntlworld.com*
Webpage: **<www.parishchest.com/>** (click on 'Parish Registers', 'Wales' and 'LandJ Research')

Williams Marriage Index for Glamorganshire.
No list of parishes survives but a list has been made up from works known and a check on the index itself. Dates give a rough guide to the period covered, i.e. 1700-1850 depending on the parish. See entry under Monmouthshire. Searches can be requested by post or in person (search by staff preferred).

The Reference Library, Newport Library and Information Service, John Frost Square, Newport, Gwent NP20 1PA.
email: *central.library@newport.gov.uk*

Glamorgan pre-1837. On CD-ROM and m'fche.
West Glamorgan Archives Service, County Hall, Swansea.

West Wales and Gower marriage bonds and fiats 1612-1800, on m'fche.
West Glamorgan Archives Service, County Hall, Swansea.

Glamorgan 1754-1875 *(Carmarthenshire FHS and Carmarthenshire Historical Society)*. Included in this index of South Wales are many baptisms, burials and other genealogical material.

Carmarthenshire FHS, PO Box 37, Aberystwyth SY23 2WL, Wales.
Webpage: **<www.carmarthenshirefhs.co.uk/>**

MERIONETH
(now part of Gwynedd)

The North Wales Marriage Index, Part 3. 100% coverage of deposited PRs supplemented by BTs and marriage bonds. Other details as Flintshire.
Dafydd Hayes, see Flintshire, page 32.

Gwynedd Marriage Index (Merioneth) 1754-1812, 1813-1837 *(Gwynedd FHS microfiche publications)*. All parishes in the county.
See under *Caernarvonshire*, page 31.

MONMOUTHSHIRE
(sometimes included with England; now **Gwent**)

Monmouthshire Marriages 1725-1812: Grooms Surname Index. Partial index, covering *c.*40% of county.
Webpage: **<freepages.genealogy.rootsweb.com/ ~monfamilies/Monmarrindex.html>**

Monmouthshire, 1754-1812 Index complete. indexed by Grooms only. Brides in the process of being indexed. All information. shown except names of witnesses. Searches free. £3 for providing details of successfully located marriage. Webpage lists names.
Webpage: **<www.mysite.freeserve.com/ MonmouthSurnames>**
Contact details as for Breconshire *1754-1812 Marriage Index*, page 31

Gwent FHS Marriage Index 1813-1837 *(Gwent FHS)*. Search service available; £1 for first 5 marriages, then 50p per marriage. Also available on CD and m'fiche. Searches from:
<www.rootsweb.com/~wlsgfhs/Services.htm>
Publications (not just 1813-37) from:
The Sales Officer, 50 Queens Hill, Newport, Gwent NP20 5HJ.
Webpage: **<www.rootsweb.com/~wlsgfhs/ Sales/Registers.htm>**
Also available from:
<www.parishchest.com>
<www.genfair.co.uk>

Williams Marriage Index for Monmouthshire and Glamorganshire. Indexed by brides and grooms surnames. Mainly alphabetical and phonetic for some surnames. Coverage: 36 parishes or about 27% of the County. Sources are mostly BTs or PR copies or printed sources. Mainly to 1812 but some parishes to 1837. Searches by post or in person (search by staff preferred). Further information from the library on request.
The Reference Library, Newport Library and Information Service, John Frost Square, Newport, Gwent NP20 1PA.

Monmouthsire 1813-37 on m'fche.
West Glamorgan Archives Service, County Hall, Swansea.

Surnames found in the Monmouthshire Marriage Index 1754-1812 Fee £3 per marriage found; less for multiple marriages.
Webpage:
<mysite.freeserve.com/MonmouthSurnames>

Non-conformist registers of Chepstow, Monmouthshire.
Index of 3,158 non-conformist baptisms, marriages, and burials mainly 19th c. Pay-per-view.
Webpage: **<www.familyhistoryonline.net/ database/GwentFHSNonCon.shtml>**

Monmouthshire *continued*

Non-parochial Marriage Announcements of Pontypool, Monmouthshire(1859-1864) *(Gwent FHS Pontypool Branch)*. Indexed transcription non-parochial marriage announcements in the *Free Press*, covering the Pontypool area. Pay-per-view.
Webpage: <www.familyhistoryonline.net/database/GwentFHSPontypoolMarA.shtml >

MONTGOMERYSHIRE
(now part of Powys)

Montgomery Parish Registers. *(Montgomeryshire Gen Soc)*. Online index; pay-per-view.
Webpage: <www.familyhistoryonline.net/database/MontgomeryGSprs.shtml>

Montgomeryshire Records *(publications from Montgomeryshire Gen Soc)*. Guisfield PC Bap/Bur/Marr 1573-1609; 1609-1642; Llanfechain PC Bap/Bur/Marr 1603-1707; 1707-1812; Llanll-wchaiarn PC Baps/Bur/Marr 1658-1730; 1813-1847 burials 1813-42 marriages 1813-37; Llansantffraid PC Bap/Bur/Marr 1582-1615; 1653-1712; Llan-santffraid Baps 1757-1838. 9 volumes.
PR/01 Mochdre PC Bap/Bur/Marr 1682-1764; PR/02 Bap/Bur1765-1812, Marr 1764-1783; PR/03 Castle Caereinion PC Bap/Marr/Bur 1663-1743; PR/05 Meifod PC Bap/Bur/Marr 1597-1648; 1649-1675; 1675-1702; PR/08 Llanllwchaiarn PC Bap/Bur/Marr 1658-1730; PR/10 1730-1812; PR/10 Bap 1813-47; Bur 1813-42; Marriages 1813-37; PR/11 Llanerfyl PC Bap/Marr/Bur 1626-1685; PR/12 1685-1735; PR/13 Marr/Bur1736-1812; PR/14 Bap1813-1857; W/01 Mochdre PC Marr 1783-1812, W/02 1813-1837, Marr 1838-1970, W.04 Banns 1824-1976; W/05 Welshpool PC Marr 1634-1754, W/06 Marr 1754-1782, W/07 Marr 1782-1812, W/08 1813-1837; W/09 Castle Caereinion PC Marr 1754-1837; W/10 Meifod PC Marr 1702-1837; W/12 Montgomery PC Marr 1754-1812.
Mr and Mrs D.F. Shirley, Maesteg, Black Bridge Lane, Llandinam, Montgomeryshire, Powys, SY17 5DJ.
Webpage: <home.freeuk.com/montgensoc/> (click on 'publications' or 'services')

Montgomeryshire marriages 1813-1837 (all) and many more before 1813. *(Montgomeryshire Genealogical Society)* There is no charge to members for searches. Apply to the librarian:
Mr Phillip B. Evans, Fronhaul, Stepaside, Mochdre, Newtown, Montgomeryshire, Powys, SY16 4JJ.

The North Wales Marriage Index, Part 3. 100% coverage of deposited PRs supplemented by BTs and marriage bonds. Other details as *Flintshire*.
Dafydd Hayes, see Flintshire, page 32.

PEMBROKESHIRE

Dyfed Marriage Index 1813-1837 *(Dyfed FHS)*. Transcripts (excl. names of witnesses) and indexes for all marriages in the whole of Dyfed (300+ parishes).
Mrs E.A. Davies, Rhydybont, Bronwydd, Carmarthen, Carmarthenshire SA33 6HX.

Pembrokeshire Marriages 1813-1837. Publication on m'fche from *Carmarthenshire FHS*.
Carmarthenshire FHS, PO Box 37, Aberystwyth, SY23 2WL.
Webpage: <www.carmarthenshirefhs.co.uk>

Pembrokeshire 1800-37 on m'fche.
West Glamorgan Archives Service, Swansea.

RADNORSHIRE
(now part of Powys)

Radnorshire Marriages pre 1754. Complete for all deposited registers. BT's for parishes where no registers survive or where there are gaps.
Dianne Foster, Mansion View, Gwystre, Llandrindod Wells, Powys, Wales LD1 6RN.

Radnorshire Marriage Index 1754-1812. Index complete. Indexed by Grooms only. Brides in the process of being indexed. All information shown except names of witnesses. Searches free. £3 for providing details of successfully located marriage. marriage found + SAE. The webpage lists names indexed.
Contact details as for Breconshire 1754-1812 Marriage Index, page 31.
Webpage: <mysite.wanadoo-members.co.uk/RadnorSurnames>

Radnorshire 1813-1837. Index complete. Indexed by grooms and brides. All information shown except names of witnesses. Searches free. £3.00 for providing details of successfully located marriage. Also available on-line, pay-per-view.
Contact details as for Breconshire 1754-1812 Marriage Index. Webpage as for Radnorshire 1754-1812 Marriage Index.
Webpage: <www.familyhistoryonline.net/database/PowellRADmar.shtml>
For a list of names in the index, visit <mysite.wanadoo-members.co.uk/RadnorSurnames> (click on 1813-1837 marriages')

Radnorshire Parish Registers on CD-ROM and booklet form. Transcripts of Baps, Banns, Marriages and Burials 1681-1901 in (Adobe pdf. format on CD-ROM) POW-PR01 CD or BK **Glascwm 1681-1901**(incl 1841-1871 census); POW-PR05CD or BK **Llanddewi Ystradenni 1732-1901**; POW-PR02 CD or BK **Llansanffraid-yn-Elfael 1701-1901** (incl. 1841-1871 census); POW-PR04 CD or BK **New-church 1755-1900** (incl. 1841-1871 census).POW-PR03 CD or BK **Winforton** (HEF) **1691-1900** (incl. 1841-1871 census).
Mr Mike MacSorley, 20 Hospital Road, Penpedairheol, Hengoed, Mid-Glam, CF82 8DG
email: m.macsorley@btopenworld.com or from <www.genfair.com> or

34

SCOTLAND

Internet Sites. There are numerous websites devoted to records of Scottish marriages. These are listed in detail in S.A. Raymond, *Scottish family history on the web: a directory.* 2nd ed. FFHS, 2006.

Scotland's People. This one pay-per-view website has digitised images of both civil registers from 1855, and Old Parish Registers 1553-1854. **<www.scotlandspeople.gov.uk/>**

BANFFSHIRE

Marriage Index. 1787-1819. Banffshire, Parish of Gamrie
Miss Margaret Shand, 52 Rio Vista Blvd, Broadbeach Waters, Queensland 4218, Australia. email: *mshand@austarnet.com.au*

DUMFRIESSHIRE

Parish of Balmaclellan. Irregular Marriages. Publication from *Dumfries and Galloway FHS.*
Dumfries and Galloway FHS, The Research Centre, 9 Glasgow St., Dumfries, DG2 9AF webpage: **<www.dgfhs.org.uk>**

Gretna Green Marriages, 1825-1855. In progress.
B. Merrell, 3912 South 2520 West, West Valley City, Utah 84119, USA.

Gretna Green. The Lang Collection of Gretna Green Marriage Records covers approximately the period 1795 (with one or two earlier entries) to 1895, in four bound and two loose second register books together with a mass of certicicates and letters. Searches are carried out at the library search rate. *IHGS, Northgate, Canterbury CT1 1BA.*
Webpage: **<www.ihgs.ac.uk>**
A surname-only commercial index is online at:
webpage: **<www.achievements.co.uk/services/gretna/index.php>**

Dumfries and Galloway. Publications from *Dumfries and Galloway FHS.*
The People of Kirkcudbright in 1786 and 1788;
Portpatrick, Wigtownshire 1759-1826;
For further details write to:
Dumfries and Galloway FHS, The Research Centre, 9 Glasgow St., Dumfries, DG2 9AF.
Webpage:
<www.dgfhs.org.uk/dgfhs/pubs/pubs-ndx.htm>

FIFE

Holy Trinity, **Dunfermline** 1840-1854; St. Peter's Episcopal, Kircaldy 1812-1854; Newburgh Associate Congregation 1821-1854; St. John's Episcopal Pittenweem 1799-1854; Rathillet Associate Congregation 1762-1840; Episcopal Church St. Andrew's 1722-1787 and 1819-1854.
Tay Valley FHS, Family History Research Centre, 179-181 Princes Street, Dundee DD4 6DQ.
website: **<www.tayvalleyfhs.org.uk/>**

IRELAND

Internet Sites. Numerous webpages are devoted to extracts, tanscripts, and indexes from Irish registers of births marriages and deaths. They are listed in detail in S.A. Raymond, *Irish family history on the web.* 3rd ed. Family History Partnership, 2007.

Irish Family History Foundation. The Foundation co-ordinates a network of government approved genealogical research centres throughout Ireland, which have computerised tens of millions of Irish ancestral records, It is planning an 'Irish Genealogical Online Record Search System', which will enable searches to be made across all of their databases.
Website: **<www.irish-roots.net/>**

Irish Church Records: Baptisms and Marriages. Small database with entries contributed by users.
Webpage: <**freepages.genealogy.rootsweb. com/~irishchurchrecords/**>

Irish Index. 15,000 birth, marriage and death announcements from *Freeman's journal,* 1817-23.
Webpage: **<www.irishindex.ca/>**

Irish Marriages: being an index to the marriages in
Walker's Hibernian Magazine **1771 to 1812.**
Index to a printed book: Henry Farrar,. *Irish Marriages Being an Index to the Marriages in Walker's Hibernian Magazine 1771 to 1812.* London: 1897.
Webpage: **<www.celticcousins.net/ ireland/irish-marriages.htm>**
A similar database is available commercially at **<www. ancestry.co.uk>**
Index to the births marriages and deaths in *Anthologia Hibernica, 1793-1794.*
Webpage: **<www.celticcousins.net/ireland/ anthologia_hibernica.htm>**

The *Belfast News Letter* was first published in 1737 and is still in circulation. **A pre-1800 index of births, marriages and deaths** recorded in the newspaper has been compiled and is available in the **Public Record Office of Northern Ireland.** In addition a complete index of surviving pre-1800 editions has also been compiled. It is available on microfiche in the **Linen Hall Library** in Belfast and also on the internet. Indexes of **births, marriages and deaths** from the *Belfast News Letter* between 1800 and 1864, and between 1945 and 1960, are also available in the Linen hall Library. Other newspapers in Northern Ireland have been partly indexed. Check with local libraries for further details. Linen Hall Library webpage:
<www.linenhall.com/genealogyAndHeraldry.asp>

Marriage Index, 1741-1845. All Protestant churches in Belfast with pre-1845 marriage registers. Minimum fee £15.
David McElroy, Irish Genealogical Services Ltd, 56 Bradbury Place, Belfast BT1 7RU, Northern Ireland.

Ireland continued

ANTRIM
Birth, Death and Marriage records for County Antrim and County Down. This online database contains a virtually complete collection of civil marriages 1845–1921, and a selection of church registers from Antrim, Down and Belfast.
<www.ancestryireland.com/
database.php?filename=db_QUIS>

ARMAGH
Armagh Ancestry Online. Online index to various civil and Roman Ctholic registers. Small fee to view records.
Webpage:

DONEGAL
Donegal Ancestry. Civil and parish register database (offline) with c.1,000,000 entries. Commercial site.
Webpage: <www.donegalancestry.com/
tracing_ancestors.php>

DOWN (*See also* Antrim)
Co. Down: Downpatrick, Newry, Banbridge Computerised records for marriages, some baptisms and some deaths – all denominations, from 1790-1920. Over 750,000 birth, marraige and death records. Fees: £15 for one search, plus £3 for a printout. The £15 required is an initial search fee whether the search is successful or not to cover costs.
Banbridge Heritage Services, Gateway Tourist Information Centre, Banbridge, BT32 3NB.
email: *info@banbridgegenealogy.com*
Webpage <www.banbridgegenealogy.com>

DUBLIN
Dublin Heritage. Webpage includes an index to Dublin parish registers.
Webpage:

FERMANAGH
Irish World Online. Commercial database (offline) covering Fermanagh and Tyrone.
Webpage: <www.donegalancestry.com/
tracing_ancestors.php>

KILDARE
Kildare History and Family Research Centre. Has computerised indexes (offline) to most Roman Catholic and Church of Ireland marriages. Fee-based.
Webpage: <kildare.ie/heritage/genealogy/
genealogical-sources.asp>

LAOIS
Irish Midlands Ancestry has an offline database, which includes church registers and civil records for Cos.Laois and Offaly. Fee-based.
Webpage:

LEITRIM
Leitrim Genealogy Centre. Index of church registers. Commercial database.
<homepage.eircom.net/%7Eleitrimgenealogy/>

LONDONDERRY
Derry Research Report Service. Indexes to Roman Catholic (pre-1900; 200,000 entries), Church of Ireland (pre-1864; 50,000 entries), and Presbyterian (pre-1864; 50,000 entries) registers; also to Co. Londonderry civil registers 1845-1921 (75,000 entries). A research report costs £75.
Website:<www.irishgenealogy.ie/csi/derry/
services/research_report/research_report.cfm>

MEATH
Meath Heritage Centre has indexes to Roman Catholic and Chuch of Ireland parish registers. Fee-based.
Webpage:

OFFALY
See Laois

TIPPERARY
Tipperary Born People Married in Victoria, Australia. Index.
Webpage: <www.from-ireland.net/vicbdms/
tipp/tippmarrs.htm>

TYRONE
See Fermanagh

CHANNEL ISLANDS
Marriage Index of Jersey 1700-1799 *(Dr. Karen Gottlieb).* Copies of this can be found at *Société Jersiaise* and *Channel Islands FHS.*

ISLE OF MAN
Registered Marriages, 1849 - 1923. This index is being prepared from m'films of the Official Indices held in the General Registry, Douglas, and from parish registers filmed by the LDS. In addition, some Roman Catholic marriages for the period 1817-1849 are included.The Roman Catholic Registers post 1849 are being transcribed.
<www.lawsons.ca/marriages/_mar_index.html>